The Story of Mexico

The Mexican Revolution

The Story of Mexico

The Mexican Revolution

R. Conrad Stein

MORGAN
REYNOLDS
PUBLISHING

Greensboro, North Carolina

The Story of Mexico

Benito Juárez and the French Intervention

The Mexican Revolution

The Mexican War of Independence

Cortés and the Spanish Conquest

THE STORY OF MEXICO
THE MEXICAN REVOLUTION

Copyright © 2008 by R. Conrad Stein

Library of Congress Cataloging-in-Publication Data

Stein, R. Conrad
  The story of Mexico. The Mexican Revolution / by R. Conrad Stein.
    p. cm.
  Includes bibliographical references and index.
  ISBN-13: 978-1-59935-051-6
  ISBN-10: 1-59935-051-3
  1. Mexico--History--Revolution, 1910-1920. I. Title. II. Title: Mexican
  Revolution.
  F1234.S85 2007
  972.08'16--dc22

                                                    2007022136

Printed in the United States of America
First Edition

For my wife Deborah and daughter, Janna

Contents

The Mexican Revolution
(Library of Congress)

ONE

Message from the Gods

L ong before Europeans came to the New World, the Aztec nation ruled central Mexico. Mystery and magic dominated Aztec thinking. The Aztecs believed that unexplainable events foretold doom for their society. Starting in the early 1500s, the people witnessed a frightening chain of dramatic and mysterious signs. A three-headed comet that baffled Aztec astronomers hung over central Mexico for many nights. An Aztec general claimed he was driven out of a northern province by stones that rained down from the sky. A temple that stood on top of the largest pyramid in the Aztec capital (present-day Mexico City) caught fire and burned to ashes despite the frantic efforts of workers to put out the blaze.

Then, in 1519 (the year One Reed on the Aztec calendar), an army of 650 Spaniards landed on Mexico's eastern shores. An ancient legend said that one day a white god would appear from the sea and claim all of Mexico as his realm. The legend predicted the god would come during the year One Reed. Commanded by Hernando Cortés, the Spaniards marched inland and captured the Aztec capital. Cortés was assisted in his conquest by the fact that, at first, many Aztecs believed he was a god. The Spanish victory was complete within two years. The mighty Aztec nation, whose territories once spread from ocean to ocean and whose armies seemed invincible, never rose again.

For the next three hundred years, the flag of Spain waved above Mexico. A new race—the mestizos—was born out of intermarriage between white Spaniards and the Aztecs and other Indian peoples. Under Spain, Mexico divided into three classes: the whites of Spanish heritage, who controlled most of the land and commanded the wealth; the mestizos, who were given meager privileges by the white ruling class; and the Indians, who were treated as a defeated race and lived in wretched poverty. A war of independence fought between 1810 and 1820 liberated Mexico from Spanish rule. But the class system, based largely on race, remained in place.

In 1910 Mexicans prepared to celebrate the one-hundredth anniversary of their War of Independence. However, from the planning stage the celebration was marred by troubling events. In Tampico a spectacular pillar of fire shot out of the ground and burned so brilliantly it could be seen for miles. American oil engineers claimed it was simply an out-of-control gusher. Over central Mexico a fiery comet lit up the night sky, frightening cows so badly they refused to give milk. Educated Mexicans knew it was Halley's Comet making its regular seventy-six year visit to Earth. But the Indians had their own explanations for the unusual occurrences. They believed, as their ancestors believed four hundred years

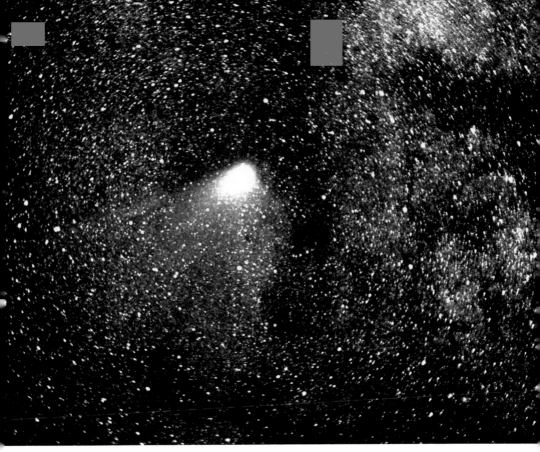

In 1910, many Mexicans thought Halley's Comet was a harbinger of war and famine. *(Courtesy of NASA)*

earlier, that these were messages from heaven and they foretold pestilence, famine, war, and death.

The Indian beliefs proved to be correct. Between 1910 and 1920 the Mexican people fought a bitter and bloody revolutionary war. It was a civil war that pitted rich against poor and white against nonwhite. During the decadelong conflict, hatred fed upon hatred and the land became a slaughterhouse. Estimates say as many as 2 million people died in the fighting and from disease and famine brought about by the conflict. The explosion of violence struck after decades of simmering frustrations and injustice. Years later the Mexican philosopher Octavio Paz described the Revolution as, "an excess and a squandering . . . an explosion of joy and hopelessness, a shout of orphanhood and jubilation, of suicide and life, all of them mingled together."

Octavio Paz (1914–1998)

Octavio Paz stands as Mexico's most famous philosopher, poet, and intellectual. He published more than forty books of poems and essays. Born in Mexico City, his grandfather was a novelist and his father once worked as a secretary to Emiliano Zapata. As a young man, Octavio Paz joined Mexico's diplomatic corps and in that capacity lived and worked in the United States, France, and India. In the 1950s, he was a declared Communist, but he grew disgusted with the dictatorial policies of the Russian leader Joseph Stalin. In 1990, Paz was awarded the distinguished Nobel Prize for literature.

TWO

The Díaz Years

After achieving independence in 1821, Mexico entered a long period of political confusion. Presidents came and went, not by free elections but through military mutinies. During that chaotic time, the gloomy general Antonio López de Santa Anna was president of Mexico eleven different times over a span of thirty years. Partly because of disorders in the capital, Mexico lost a disastrous war with the United States in 1848. As a result of the war, Mexico was forced to give up all its northern territories including the present-day American states of New Mexico, Arizona, and California. The loss of California was made even more grievous in 1849 when gold was discovered and instantly transformed that once sleepy place into a prosperous American state.

The nation also endured a four-year occupation by the French. But here the Mexican people rallied behind President Benito Juárez. President Juárez was a full-blooded Zapotec Indian, the first of his race to achieve the office of president.

1839 map of Mexico

With stubborn determination, Juárez fought the French intervention in Mexico. French forces withdrew, and the European nobleman Maximilian, who served as emperor, was executed by firing squad in the city of Querétaro in June of 1867.

After the French defeat, Benito Juárez tried to bring democracy and progress to Mexico, but Juárez died of a heart attack in 1872. His death triggered five years of strife and military manipulation as rivals fought for the presidential chair.

In 1876, Juárez's onetime military commander, Porfirio Díaz, became president. Díaz grew up in the southern state of Oaxaca. He was a mestizo of mostly Mixtec Indian blood. His family ran a tiny hotel. As a boy the future president admired the army officers who paraded through his town,

Benito Juárez led the fight against French occupation of Mexico.
(Library of Congress)

riding the finest horses he had ever seen. Early in life Díaz decided to make the army his career. While serving as a junior officer, he proved fearless under fire. Díaz was captured in the war against the French, but he made a daring escape and returned to lead his unit.

Upon becoming president, Díaz took command of a country significantly out of step with the rest of the modern world. While Europe and the United States had developed extensive factory systems, Mexico lacked even a modern railroad. Latin nations such as Brazil, Argentina, Chile, and Cuba were worlds ahead of Mexico in industrial progress. Nearly six decades of warfare had cost Mexico its place among the industrial nations. Now Díaz intended to keep the peace in order to build a bright future for his country.

Porfirio Díaz became president of Mexico in 1876. *(Library of Congress)*

To end the savage military mutinies that led to internal wars, Díaz offered his rivals the choice of *pan o palo* (bread or the club). In effect, he told ambitious politicians and generals: Work with me and you will be rewarded; fight me and you will be beaten down. Ruthlessly and without hesitation he killed military men intent on taking his place as president. When a group of army officers attempted to overthrow him in the 1880s, he issued a simple order, "Kill them on the spot." Still, for the most part, political executions were rare in the Díaz years. Ambitious political leaders were put on the government payroll and provided with a handsome salary because, as Díaz was fond of saying, "A dog with a bone in his mouth neither bites nor barks."

Díaz's political strength grew to envelop the entire nation. Soon all twenty-seven of Mexico's state governors were Díaz's hand-chosen men. Elections were held, but the president's small army of *jefes-poíiticos* (political bosses) stuffed ballot boxes and rigged results. In one state, prisoners were put to work marking ballots and sending them to vote counters. Díaz also exercised absolute control over the congress in Mexico City. Once he gratefully presented a seat in the House of Deputies to a dentist who had cured his aching tooth. Democracy, Díaz believed, was an empty dream in a country where only 15 percent of the people could read and write. But instead of investing in education, Díaz steered his nation relentlessly toward industrialization. Public schools for the masses would simply have to wait. First Díaz wanted to build factories and railroads.

Under the president's rule, Mexico finally joined the industrial age. During his time in office, more than 9,000 miles of railroad tracks were laid. The output of mines increased threefold, and the value of goods Mexico shipped abroad registered a fivefold gain. Steel plants opened in Nuevo León and textile factories operated in Veracruz. The production of manufactured goods more than doubled, meaning that Mexico now stood on the brink of becoming a modern industrialized nation.

Agriculture too took giant steps forward under Díaz. New laws encouraged the growth of huge plantations, which produced sugar, coffee, tobacco, cotton, and rubber. The cattle business thrived on huge ranches in Mexico's north. In the early 1900s the production of cotton and sugar increased by 100 percent. Mexico became a leading exporter of henequen fiber which is used in making rope.

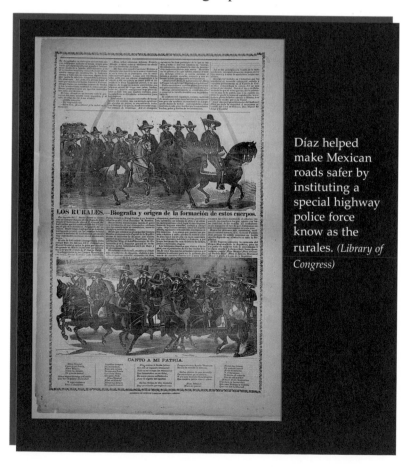

Díaz helped make Mexican roads safer by instituting a special highway police force know as the rurales. *(Library of Congress)*

Commerce could not develop efficiently without improved transportation. Mexican roads were feared for the bandit gangs which stormed over the highway network, terrorizing coach passengers and stealing freight. Employing ironfisted policies, Díaz subdued the bandits by turning the toughest highway men into police. Supplied with smart uniforms, silver badges, and menacing-looking broad brimmed hats, the onetime highway pirates became the famed rurales (rural police). Using methods learned through a lifetime of banditry, the rurales gave Mexico safe roads. By law rurales were forbidden to execute prisoners, but they were allowed to shoot suspects who they claimed were fleeing custody. During the Díaz years many hundreds of would-be bandits were reported "killed while attempting to escape."

Nine out of ten Mexicans lived in farming communities in the Díaz era. The most explosive problem facing the president was land ownership, an issue almost as old as Mexico itself. Under Spain, farmland was divided mostly into ejidos owned by Indians and haciendas owned by Europeans. Ejidos were tracts of land that were either worked by all of the people of the village or were subdivided into tiny plots and assigned to individual farmers. Haciendas were sprawling farms or ranches owned by one rich family. A single hacienda often spread over 10,000 acres and employed more than one hundred field hands.

Díaz believed that haciendas were more efficient than ejidos, and he allowed wealthy land barons to strip millions of acres from Indian villages. To take over ejido land, hacienda owners twisted the intent of an 1856 law that was designed to break up large estates owned by the Catholic church. Indian

In the southern region of Mexico, Emiliano Zapata led a revolt to reclaim the land taken away from small farmers. *(Courtesy of AP Images)*

villages fought the haciendas in court, but won few cases in a system where judges owed their jobs to the whims of Porfirio Díaz.

In the south frustrated Indians who lost their land to the haciendas and large plantations sought help from a young farmer named Emiliano Zapata. Under the banner of "land and liberty," Zapata began a revolt designed to restore the rights and dignity of small farmers. Northern ranch hands and farmers turned to a onetime highway bandit and

Pancho Villa *(Library of Congress)*

cattle thief named Pancho Villa. Warfare was a way of life to Villa, who had long fought law authorities and rival bandits. These rebellions or resistance movements, led by Villa and Zapata, marked the beginnings of the great Mexican Revolution of 1910-1920.

Still other Mexicans fought the system by escaping to the north. For generations Mexicans seeking work migrated to

Mexican refugees crossing the Rio Grande *(Library of Congress)*

Modern Migrants

Today more than 1 million Mexican and other Latin American workers cross the U.S. border legally and illegally each year. As was true one hundred years ago, the migrants are motivated by economics. Jobs commonly pay six to eight dollars an hour in the United States, whereas on the Mexican side of the border the same work pays six to eight dollars a day.

the United States. At the turn of the twentieth century the number of migrants soared. Exact figures are not known, but it appears that fewer than one thousand Mexicans crossed the border in 1902. Then, because of the land upheavals at home, more than 15,000 Mexicans entered the United States in the first six months of 1909. Many Mexican workers made friends with American socialists, who were at the time strong political activists. Mexican migrants published a newspaper, *Regeneración*, which urged Mexicans at home to join labor unions and farmer's organizations. The newspaper was printed irregularly because the writers were often in U.S. jails, put there along with their socialist friends for promoting radical politics.

William Randolph Hearst *(Library of Congress)*

Díaz's policies gave the countryside hoards of landless people along with some of the world's largest privately owned farms. The Terrazas family in the state of Chihuahua owned more than 7 million acres. The Cedros clan of Zacatecas lived on a hacienda that sprawled over almost 4 million acres. Foreigners frequently bought land that the government had taken from Indians. The American newspaper tycoon and cattle breeder William Randolph Hearst owned a ranch in northern Mexico that was said to be the size of both Maryland and Delaware combined. By contrast, the numbers of landless poor Mexicans increased every year. In 1895, 20 percent of the Mexican people owned at least

As more and more farmers lost their land, many families were forced to relocate to shacks in the slums of Mexico City. *(Library of Congress)*

a small plot of land or a share in an ejido; in 1910 only 2 percent claimed to be landowners.

The expropriation of Indian lands set in motion protests and shooting wars. Following Díaz's orders, the rurales and the army brutally crushed all attempts at rebellion. In the state of Hidalgo, the rurales buried Indian protesters neck-deep in the ground and then galloped over their heads with horses. To protect their land, the Yaqui Indians of Sonora barricaded themselves in the hills. Cash bounties were awarded to anyone bringing in a Yaqui ear or hand. Finally the Yaquis were starved out of their mountain hideouts.

The governor of Sonora, Ramón Corral—who later became Díaz's vice president—ordered all Yaqui leaders shot. Many farmers, robbed of their land, drifted into the cities hoping to find some sort of job so they could feed their families. The outskirts of Mexico City became urban slums. The poor lived in shacks made from discarded building material. Shack towns holding three hundred or more families were jammed into an area the size of a football field. Running water, sewers, and toilets did not exist in the shacktowns. Half the babies born in the poor areas died before their first birthday.

A new class of landless peasants grew in rural Mexico. These farmers without farms were exploited by large hacienda owners who ran what amounted to slave camps. Hacienda owners induced jobless farmers to sign contracts promising their labor for at least a year. The illiterate farmers had no way of knowing they were signing into a form of slavery. In the camps workers had no choice but to buy food from the company store and worship at the company-owned church. The company stores, the hated *tiendas rayas*, charged far more for food and other goods than did stores outside the camp.

Plantation owners deducted from a worker's pay any debts he had at the company store. Clothing, housing, and other expenses such as "legal fees" were also deducted. Even the signing of a labor contract called for a legal fee, though the worker never saw a lawyer. Because of debts and other deductions a worker's payday at the end of each month was miniscule, and he was often given a statement declaring debt instead of the cash wages expected.

The country's most notorious labor camp was the Valle Nacional (National Valley), a huge tobacco plantation in the state of Oaxaca. At least 15,000 new workers were herded into the Valle Nacional each year. About 10 percent of the labor force was made up of prisoners who had committed petty crimes or were jailed as political troublemakers. Politicians sold the convicts to plantation owners for $45 a head. Defeated Yaqui Indians were frequently sent to the gigantic tobacco plantation. But most of the workers were free Mexican campesinos (farmers) who signed labor contracts because they desperately needed a job. In the Valle Nacional the workers were forced to pick tobacco under the blistering sun, sleep amid swarms of mosquitoes, and live on a near-starvation diet. Escape through the jungles and mountains that ringed the valley was impossible. A worker who failed to please his bosses was tied to the camp whipping post and lashed.

The American writer John Kenneth Turner interviewed a Valle Nacional field boss who claimed, "By the sixth or seventh month they [the workers] begin to die off like flies at the first winter frost. . . . The cheapest thing to do is to let them die; there are plenty more where they came from . . . I have been here more than five years and every month I see hundreds and sometimes thousands of men, women, and children start over the road to the valley, but I never see them come back."

Hacienda hired hands fared little better than the contract laborers. Many fieldworkers lost their farms to the ever-expanding haciendas. They then had to work for the hacienda, often tilling the same soil that had been owned (they thought) by their families for generations. As was true with the contract laborers, the hacienda workers ran up debts that could not be repaid in a lifetime. Debts were passed from

The Mysterious B. Traven

B. Traven was a writer who lived with the impoverished people of rural Mexico in the early twentieth century. He was also a mystery man. Traven might have been an American born in Chicago in 1890, or he might have been a Swiss or a German born in Europe in 1882. He wrote in both German and English. Traven used several different names, and he refused to be interviewed by anyone. His most famous book is *Treasure of the Sierra Madre*, which in 1947 became a movie starring Humphrey Bogart as a gold miner in Mexico who goes mad with greed. Some of Traven's most powerful books describe the terrible conditions in southern Mexico's farm areas. Traven writes in a crude manner, but his books have a raw power that makes them compelling. In *Rebellion of the Hanged* he tells of workers in a logging camp who were punished by being hung by their hands to trees and left there to be tormented by swarms of mosquitoes. In the book a new worker reports to the logging camp and hears distant screams. A veteran worker tells him, "It's twenty cutters, twenty axmen who are howling. They've hung them up there for three or four hours because they haven't produced [the four tons] of mahogany they'd been told to. You are innocent and ignorant, but within three days you'll know what four tons are. "Over the years, Traven's books have sold more than 25 million copies, and his works have been translated into thirty languages.

B. Traven's popularity has faded in the United States recently, although he still has a band of loyal readers. Books by B. Traven remain required reading in many Mexican schools today.

father to son so that babies were born owing the hacienda their labor. Escaping the hacienda was a criminal offense since it meant running out on debt payments. Although they were free Mexican citizens, the workers were commonly whipped by the hacienda owners for a multitude of offenses. Stealing even the smallest item of hacienda-owned property was punishable by two hundred lashes. In most, this led to death.

President Díaz was aware of the conditions in rural Mexico and in the cities. Journalists had written dozens of reports about the horrors of the labor camps. It was said that Díaz wept upon hearing of one Indian village losing its ejido land to the haciendas. But the president was determined to march Mexico into a new age of industrial and agricultural efficiency. Ejidos were an old-fashioned institution. He believed modern and efficient haciendas were the wave of the future. His many political allies agreed with the president and were quick to heap praise upon him. In 1905, the congress granted Porfirio Díaz a special medal with a gold-and-jewel inscription reading, "He pacified and united the nation."

The policies of President Díaz took a new twist in 1900 when Díaz fell under the influence of a small group of businessmen called the científicos (scientists). Headed by Finance Minister José Limantour, the científicos believed the problems of government and the national economy could be solved by the proper application of scientific principles.

For example, the científicos concluded that Mexico needed foreign investment if it was to continue on the road toward industrial development. Foreign investors sought low wages, low taxes, no labor unrest, and subsidies from the government. The científicos assured foreign interests they would find all of these blessings in Mexico.

The cientificos, whites whose families had arrived from Europe since Independence, believed Indians and mestizos were suitable for manual labor only. Therefore, they allowed American and European companies to bring in all the skilled personnel they wished. The Indians and mestizos, who comprised 90 percent of the population of Mexico in 1910, were relegated to only the lowliest jobs. White workers from Europe and the United States earned two and three times more than the pay granted to native Mexicans. The abuses committed by foreign interests led to watchwords which were repeated often in the revolutionary fighting to come: "Mexico For The Mexicans."

Until the rise of the cientificos, Díaz had ruled dictatorially, but he ruled like a Mexican. His cabinet ministers and the businessmen he favored included many mestizos and some Indians. Yet Díaz—who was himself of mostly Indian blood—acceded to the white, pro-foreign policies of the científicos. Díaz retained full control of the government, but he allowed the economy to be taken over by the científicos and the foreign investors. Soon American companies ran Mexico's railroads and owned three-quarters of its mines and more than half of its oil fields. American commitment to Mexico grew to $1 billion, which was even more than Mexican businesses had invested in their country. Foreign firms came to own one-third of the Mexican economy. British interests acquired gold and silver mines. The French operated the textile mills. Spaniards owned tobacco and coffee plantations. A popular saying throughout the country went, "Mexico—mother of foreigners, stepmother of Mexicans."

The arrival of foreign businesses provided jobs but did little to improve the lives of Mexican workers. To the científicos a horse was the same as a man inasmuch as both performed work. A leading científico, Francisco Bulnes declared,

"Nothing is just or unjust as far as profit is concerned. Labor is a product like any other, such as corn, wheat, flour, and is subject to the law of supply and demand."

Survival of the fittest was the guiding principle of the científicos. In a 1901 speech, the cientifico Limantour said, "The weak, the unprepared, those who lack the necessary tools to triumph in the evolutionary process, must perish and leave the field to the strongest."

The sudden influx of foreign money raised the prices of corn, beans, and other staples of the Mexican diet. Many fields that once grew corn and beans were taken over by foreign companies and now produced beef cattle for the American market or coffee to be exported to Europe. Mexico, for the first time in its history, had to import corn from the United States and pay premium prices for the crop. These pressures made the price of simple tortillas soar in Mexican marketplaces. But, as the científicos had promised, Mexican workers' wages remained low. Labor unions were broken up by local police or by the army. In terms of the price of corn, the average Mexican earned less in 1910 than in 1810. Human labor became so cheap that it cost more per day to rent a mule than it did to hire a man.

In office, Díaz grew graceful and respected with age. After his wife died, he married the eighteen-year-old daughter of a wealthy Mexico City businessman. Cultured and dignified, she taught the president certain niceties, such as the proper knife and fork to use with each course served at a formal dinner. The president's young wife also busied herself with civic projects such as planting trees along Mexico City's broad boulevards.

Because of Mexico's industrial progress, leaders in world capitals heaped praise upon Porfirio Díaz. In many respects the praise was justified. He was the only government figure since Independence strong enough to end the barracks rebellions that had thrown the country into anarchy. He had taken Mexico out of debt and brought in factories to a once undeveloped land. American president Theodore Roosevelt suggested that Washington could use an administrator as accomplished as Díaz.

As the year 1910 approached, many observers believed Mexico had at last achieved stability and a degree of economic prosperity. In 1909, the Mexico City newspaper *El Imparcial* declared, "A revolution in Mexico is impossible."

THREE

The Gathering Storm

T he Paseo de la Reforma is a broad, treelined boulevard that cuts through the heart of Mexico City. In 1910, the Reforma was the capital's showcase street. Statues and fountains, most of them erected during the Díaz years, decorated the boulevard. At nearby Alameda Park construction workers were building a grand opera house, made of Italian marble and a pet project of Díaz's wife. On other downtown streets automobiles chugged alongside brightly polished horse-drawn carriages. Electric streetcars carried shoppers and office workers. People walking past the display windows of department stores wore the latest suits and dresses from Paris and London. Europeans visiting the capital hailed it as "the Paris of the New World."

The Elegant Reforma

The Paseo de La Reforma, often simply called La Reforma, is named after an important period in Mexican history called the Reform Movement. During the late 1850s, President Benito Juárez led the Reform Movement, stripping the Catholic Church of the power it once had over the lives and the government of the Mexican people.

Many other streets and highways in Mexican towns are named Reforma, but none has the glamour of the Mexico City boulevard. Construction of the capital's Reforma Boulevard began in the 1860s under orders of Emperor Maximilian who wanted to create the feel of Paris in Mexico City. The Díaz administration spent millions of pesos to decorate and widen the boulevard. Today the Paseo de La Reforma is flanked with luxury high-rise apartment buildings and remains the most elegant avenue in the country.

Mexico City's charming central district masked other ugly sides of the capital. Not far from the central plaza, the Zócalo, stood shacktowns and slums. In the poverty stricken slums, infant mortality was high, and boys and girls who survived shacktown life and reached the age of five never saw the inside of a classroom. The científicos claimed the Mexican budget must be used to foster industry and could not be diverted to fund schools for the poor.

Twice a day the aging Porfirio Díaz took a long coach ride down the Paseo de la Reforma to the National Palace at the Zócalo. Police were especially diligent to clear the streets of beggars during the hours of the president's daily rides. He had changed, drastically, from his days as a leather-tough cavalry officer. Thanks to the influence of his young wife, Díaz now wore only the most tasteful suits which were impeccably

The opera house in Alameda Park during its construction *(Library of Congress)*

tailored. His gray handlebar mustache was barbered every morning. He had grown to enjoy parties and balls, especially those hosted by the foreign community.

Except for a four-year period in the 1880s, Díaz held office for thirty-four years. Most observers assumed the presidency was his till death. But in 1908, Díaz granted an interview to the American newsman James Creelman and said, "No matter what my friends and supporters say, I retire when my presidential term of office ends [in 1910], and I shall not serve again. . . . I welcome an opposition party in the Mexican Republic. If it appears I will regard it as a blessing, not an evil."

The Creelman interview created a sensation. Never before had Díaz indicated he would step down, and not once had he hinted he would tolerate an opposing political party. In the previous two elections, the only person to dare run against

Díaz was a lunatic who roamed the streets of Mexico City warning of the coming of tidal waves and adding, almost as an afterthought, that he was a candidate for president.

By 1910, however, Díaz acted as if the Creelman interview had never taken place. He announced he would be a candidate for reelection and he suppressed rival parties with his customary harshness. It is a mystery why he told James Creelman he would retire and he would support free elections. Perhaps when he granted the interview he was musing about retirement and then simply changed his mind. Or perhaps he was telling an American reporter what he thought an American audience wanted to hear. Nevertheless, the interview excited the hopes of intellectuals, labor leaders, and journalists who had long ago tired of Díaz's dictatorial rule. Those dissidents were willing to support anyone bold enough to stand up to the president. In the northern state of Coahuila, they found their candidate.

Francisco Madero came from an old hacienda-owning family. He was one of the wealthiest men in Mexico. Early in the Díaz administration, his grandfather was a state governor and an ally of the president. Despite his family's wealth and influence, Madero was genuinely concerned with the plight of the poor. From his own pocket he paid for the education of his farmworkers' children. He often fed peasant children at the huge dining room table in his hacienda manor house.

Thin, balding, and standing only five feet two inches tall, Madero looked more like a kindly schoolteacher than a political leader. His voice was squeaky, almost birdlike. Many of his personal habits were unusual for the period. In an age when most wealthy men drank brandy and puffed cigars, Madero refused to touch alcohol or tobacco. He was also a

Francisco Madero *(Library of Congress)*

strict vegetarian. He practiced a spiritual form of religion, and in times of great personal despair claimed he was able to speak with the soul of his dead brother.

For years Madero had taken a scholarly interest in politics. In 1908 he wrote a book urging free elections in Mexico. With anti-Díaz sentiment on the rise, the book was well received. Madero soon had a small but loyal following among the educated middle class. At first Díaz refused to take Madero's opposition seriously. He met with Madero but later told jokes about the vegetarian dreamer. The clash between the two men pitted the old against the new. Madero was thirty-seven years old and had never held political office. Díaz was almost eighty and had been president for the better part of thirty years. No one, Díaz believed, would take Madero seriously.

Then, in early 1910, Madero's campaign gained momentum. Crowds swelled as he crisscrossed the country making speeches. His audience grew to include not only the intellectuals and the middle class but also debt-ridden farm workers. Some of the campesinos who listened to Madero had backs scarred by the hacienda whip. Díaz, alarmed by the sudden attention Madero was receiving, reacted in a predictable manner. He had Madero thrown in jail on trumped-up charges.

Election Day, June 21, 1910, was ordinary. Díaz

Ramón Corral (*Library of Congress*)

won by a huge majority. Earlier the only suspense had been over whom Díaz would choose as his vice president. Insiders speculated it would be José Limantour, the leading cientifico. Díaz surprised the experts by picking Ramón Corral, who recently had earned a fortune selling the defeated Yaqui people into slavery in the labor camps. Corral was one of the most hated men in Mexico, and some believed Díaz chose him as a form of life insurance. Only a fool would assassinate Díaz with Corral next in line to be president.

In Mexico City the great celebration of September 16 began. On that date one hundred years earlier, Miguel Hidalgo, a gentle and bookish priest in the town of Dolores, rang the

Miguel Hidalgo y Costilla

church bell to summon his Indian parishioners to Mass. In the churchyard the priest issued the renowned *Grito de Dolores* (Cry of Dolores). With that one speech, the Mexican War of Independence—the proudest chapter in the country's history—was launched.

The Paseo de la Reforma served as the parade ground to honor the first famous Grito. Coincidently, Porfirio Díaz's eightieth birthday fell one day before the September 16 Independence celebration. So the festivities honored both Independence and the president's birthday. Never had the Reforma Boulevard looked so resplendent as a parade stretching for miles wound by. A half-million Mexican citizens crowded the sidewalks to watch. They cheered the folk dancers and the floats that depicted Mexican history back to Aztec times. They applauded the many marching bands.

As entertainment, the parade was a smashing success. But a certain energy was absent during this combined presidential birthday and Independence celebration. Widespread poverty and fear of uprisings on the farms and in the cities drained the Mexican people of their festive spirit. Recently labor strikes had rocked the railroad industry and several factories. Such strikes were unheard of earlier in the Díaz regime. The revolutionaries Zapata and Villa continued their guerilla wars in the countryside. Well-to-do Mexicans worried about the country's stability and many secretly blamed the policies of the eighty-year-old president for the unrest. A strange, almost eerie hush overcame the spectators when the open car bearing Díaz drove past. An American reporter wrote, "Thousands thronged to watch the passing show, yet there was no outburst of delight. Porfirio Díaz, brilliant with royal decorations . . . swept by without applause."

Francisco Madero had been imprisoned in San Luis Potosí in northern Mexico. After the independence celebrations, Díaz released Madero from jail but forbade him from traveling beyond the city limits of San Luis Potosí. His time spent in jail had jarred Madero's thinking. Throughout his life he had shunned violence. But clearly Porfirio Díaz would accept no peaceful, democratic change in Mexico. Madero was now convinced that only armed rebellion could topple Díaz from power. He prayed that if a revolutionary war swept Mexico it would be short and the bloodshed minimal.

Madero's supporters secretly ushered him across the border to Laredo, Texas. From Texas he issued the Plan of San Luis Potosi, a course of action he conceived while sitting in his prison cell. This was the first of many "plans" devised by revolutionary figures and designed to steer Mexico into a new era of prosperity and peace. The Plan of San Luis Potosi declared the recent Díaz election to be fraudulent and illegal and urged Mexicans to take up arms on November 20, 1910, to demand the president step down from office. This call to arms was a radical and dangerous step for the peace-loving Madero to make. November 20 came and went. Except for a minor clash in the city of Puebla, no mass uprising broke out. Madero lacked a strong enough following to produce a revolution on demand.

Despite the failed uprising, the resistance movements led by Villa and Zapata grew stronger. The two totally unconnected rebellions that gained fury in 1910 were anti-rich rather than pro-Madero. They were the opening dark clouds of the great storm about to strike Mexico.

In the rugged northern state of Chihuahua, Pancho Villa began a series of devastating raids on wealthy cattle ranches.

Villa (fifth from the left) stands with a group of his soldiers. *(Library of Congress)*

Villa's horse soldiers were made up of landless Indians and underpaid mestizo miners, all of whom hated their wealthy bosses. To finance his operations, Villa rustled cattle and used the proceeds to buy guns.

To the south, in the state of Morelos, the farmworkers' revolt grew in intensity under the leadership of Emiliano Zapata. The campesinos of Morelos sought to reclaim the land that was theirs before the expansion of the haciendas. Few of the campesinos could read or write, but all could ride and shoot. Zapata's men stormed haciendas, stole cattle and horses, and slipped away into the night.

Initially the movements led by Villa and Zapata appeared to be minor upheavals that would soon die out. But instead of ebbing, the rebellions expanded in armed force and military spirit.

Zapata (seated, middle) poses with a group of his campesino soldiers. *(Library of Congress)*

The first warriors of the Mexican Revolution identified closely with their leaders. Thus Villa's men called themselves the Villistas, while the soldiers of Zapata were known as the Zapatistas. The practice of naming troops after their commanders continued in the later years, when the Mexican Revolution became more a conflict of personalities than a battle of ideals.

From Mexico City, Díaz sent armies to Morelos and to the north with orders to snuff out the rebellions. The army units had little success against the hit-and-run Villistas and Zapatistas, who knew every twist and bend in the country roads. In Morelos the Zapatistas took over plantation lands and defended them against the federal armies. The governor of Morelos, who was chased out of the state by the Zapatistas, echoed the growing fear of Mexico's establishment when he told a friend, "These are difficult times . . . The peasant is now the master."

In the north the Villistas captured the important railway center of the city of Chihuahua. The victory in that city allowed Madero to recross the border and enter Mexico. At Chihuahua, Madero the idealist met Villa the outlaw for the first time. Madero, a white, was a rich hacienda owner. Villa, a mestizo, was the son of a lowly hacienda worker.

Despite their conflicting backgrounds, the two men developed a friendship based on mutual respect. Villa looked upon Madero as a vital political and intellectual leader of the revolution that was brewing in the land. He also genuinely liked the man. He once said of Madero, "Here is one rich man who fights for the people. He is a little fellow, but he has a great soul. If all the rich and powerful in Mexico were like him, there would be no struggle . . ." Madero recognized Villa as a gifted military commander and chose to ignore the stories that he heard about the man's cruel, often murderous moods. However, Madero quickly learned he could not control the bandit chief. He ordered Villa to stay put at Chihuahua, but the outlaw brazenly ignored the order and marched north to even greater plunder.

At the border city of Ciudad Juárez, a bloody house-to-house battle broke out between the Villistas and the federal army defenders. The Villistas were armed with rifles that were relics of past wars. One of their artillery pieces was a seventy-year-old cannon that had been stolen from the courthouse lawn in El Paso, Texas. Despite their primitive weapons, Villa and his men displayed reckless courage and battlefield initiative that would become their signature in the combat to come. When the Villistas found the narrow streets barricaded by federal troops, they dynamited buildings to clear a path for their advance. Often they broke into one house and then used picks and axes to chop down the walls to the neighboring house and in this way continued their house-to-house march.

The city of Ciudad Juárez lies across the Rio Grande from El Paso, Texas. During the height of the fighting, thousands of Americans gathered on El Paso rooftops to watch. Some of the American onlookers placed bets on the results of the many swirling street battles going on below them. Their sport ended when several Americans were wounded by stray bullets.

Villistas stand beside a cannon after taking control of Ciudad Juárez. *(Library of Congress)*

On May 10, 1911, the federal commander of Ciudad Juárez surrendered. Villa gave orders to execute the commander, but at the last minute Madero saved the man's life by escorting him across the border into Texas. The fall of Ciudad Juárez was decisive. From that city Madero and Villa could supply their forces with modern guns bought in from the United States. The victory also ignited uprisings in dozens of smaller villages and hamlets.

In his mansion on the Paseo de la Reforma, President Díaz bent over maps spread on his favorite billiard table. Furiously he telegraphed orders to the fighting fronts. Now and then he raged about his officers' inability to put down a few revolutionary bandits. At one point the eighty-one year-old president and ex-army officer told his aides he would ride out to the field and personally take command of the troops.

While Díaz fussed over the military situation, the day-to-day functions of government fell to Limantour, the top cientifico. Limantour was above all a realist who shunned military adventures. With Madero and Villa commanding the north and the rampaging Zapatistas tearing up the state of Morelos in the south, the government's position seemed hopeless. Adding to the government's peril were the angry crowds that gathered every evening on the Zócalo below the National Palace. From his office window Limantour heard their menacing chants: "Death to Díaz. Death to the cientificos. Death to Díaz!"

Limantour sent an emissary to Madero asking for terms of peace. Madero and the Limantour representative met in the countryside near Ciudad Juárez on the night of May 21, 1911. On a folding table illuminated by car headlights,

The Historic Zócalo

One of the largest public plazas in the world, the Zócalo lies in the heart of Mexico City. Even in Aztec times the grounds were a religious center and a gathering spot. The tallest pyramid in the Aztec capital stood where the National Cathedral, built by the Spaniards, rises today. The word Zócalo means base of a statue. In the mid-1800s the government put the base of a statue on the plaza grounds, but then government leaders argued endlessly as to whose statue should be put on the base. Meanwhile the people began to call the plaza the Zócalo, after the statue base.

Finally the base, which was never graced with a statue, was removed. Today the Zócalo is the political and the spiritual center of Mexico. Young couples come to the plaza to get married. Striking school teachers and other workers come to shout protests.

the two parties signed an agreement. Díaz and Limantour would resign. Vice President Corral was no longer a factor, because he had escaped into exile at the first sign of trouble. Francisco de la Barra, the Mexican ambassador to the United States, was to serve as interim president until new elections could be held. The favorite candidate in such elections was clearly Francisco Madero. News of the agreement electrified Mexico City. Crowds gathered at the Zócalo, and in front of the president's mansion. People banged on oilcans and yelled for Díaz's immediate resignation. A group of young men broke into a chant that had grown popular with the city's labor unions:

Little work, lots of dinero (money)
Beans for all—Viva Madero!

Tragedy struck the Zócalo when panic-stricken troops fired into the mob. The demonstrators fled and a sudden rain drenched the plaza. Onlookers peering out of windows counted two hundred corpses strewn about the Zócalo, their blood running in rain-driven rivulets.

Just before sunrise on May 26, President Díaz—now showing his age—was helped into a limousine. At his side was his young

After the resignation of Díaz and Limantour, Francisco de la Barra was chosen to be interim president of Mexico. *(Library of Congress)*

wife. The two were rushed to the railway station, where they boarded a train for the port city of Veracruz. There a ship took them to exile in France. Díaz died in Paris four years later. Before he left the country he had ruled for more than a third of a century, he told a friend, "They [the revolutionaries] have turned the mares loose—let's see who can corral again."

A triumphant Francisco Madero entered Mexico City in early June 1911. Joyous crowds shouting, "Viva Madero!" and "Viva la Revolución!" filled the streets. The over-whelming majority of the people had never seen the little politician or heard him speak. Still they hailed Madero as a saint, a savior delivered by God with orders to uplift their nation. Perhaps the spiritualist Madero also thought he was on a divine mission. He had prayed that the revolution, should it come, would be short and the blood spilled minimal. So far the death and violence prompted by revolutionary passions had been shocking but not widespread. Could it be that God had answered Madero's prayers?

An ominous note dampened the festivities. Almost the moment Madero stepped off the train on June 7, 1911, a sharp earthquake rocked the capital. The quake sent thousands of terrified residents streaming into the streets. A musician thought the earthquake was a positive sign and wrote a song that became popular:

> Quando Madero llego/ hasta la tierra temblo
> (When Madero arrived/ even the earth trembled)

But for many people, especially the Indians, the earthquake held a mystic and somber significance. It was a message from the heavens saying the terrible winds sweeping Mexico would not diminish. In fact, the winds of war would become a hurricane.

FOUR

Madero

By early 1911 Francisco Madero was the most popular man in Mexico. Wherever he traveled, he was greeted by excited crowds, brass bands, and children strewing flowers at his feet. If he wished, Madero could simply have taken over the office of president without waiting for elections to be held. But Madero was true to his word. He had agreed to let the interim government run the country until October, when organized elections were scheduled. As a champion of democracy, he would under no circumstances become president until he was legitimately elected to that office.

A tense period passed as Mexicans waited for the elections. The nation was still in a state of revolution, and armed peasant bands remained at the ready in the countryside. The interim president, Francisco de la Barra, ordered the rebel armies to lay down their rifles, but his directions were ignored. In the north, Pancho Villa remained aligned with Madero. To show his support for the incoming president, Villa curtailed the activities of his army. The Revolution, which had been a fire, now smoldered as Madero campaigned for votes.

Elections took place as planned in October. Madero was swept into office, winning more than 90 percent of the votes cast. He had chosen José María Pino Suárez, a journalist from the state of Yucatán, to be his vice president. Madero and Pino Suárez took their oaths of office on November 6, 1911. At last the Mexican people enjoyed a freely elected president and vice president.

Although Madero won more than 90 percent of the votes cast in the 1911 presidential election, he quickly lost popular support. *(Library of Congress)*

Madero soon learned he had inherited a nation he was unable to govern. In the countryside the campesinos demanded land that the hacienda owners refused to relinquish. In the cities laborers clamored for a living wage, while profit-minded businessmen rejected their requests. To the burning demands for land and bread, Madero offered only philosophy. As president he believed his one overriding mission was to make Mexico a democratic country. Once democracy was fully established, he reasoned, the nation's other problems would be settled by mutual agreements reached with all parties. This belief ignored the grim facts that most Mexicans were poorly fed, ill clothed, and slept in mud hovels. Moreover, Madero refused to recognize the economic emergency his nation faced. The president once told a reporter, "The Mexican people are not asking me for bread, they are asking me for liberty."

In office, Madero talked about reforms such as land redistribution, but his talk rarely translated into action. He turned the question of land redistribution over to a committee made up of congressmen. The committee never issued a significant report on the problem. Yet by simply talking about rights for workers and land for peasants, Madero stepped on powerful toes. Hacienda owners, mine owners, and foreign businessmen began to brand him as a dangerous radical. The president was caught in crossfire between the political right and the political left. In just a matter of months, the once widely popular Madero lost much of his support.

The Mexico City press lambasted the new president. The liberal newspapers complained that he was sitting on his hands on the land issue, while the conservative press denounced him as being antibusiness. As the president's popularity sagged, the newspapers continued their campaign against his government. One cartoonist portrayed Madero as a figure flattened on the pavement, and at the figure's head was a steamroller labeled PUBLIC OPINION.

The explosive issue of land ownership simply would not disappear in a swell of democratic energy as the president hoped it would. The status of hacienda workers remained the same under Madero as it was under Díaz. The workers were deeply in debt, and they often tilled the same fields that were owned by their fathers and grandfathers before the Díaz government spurred the expansion of haciendas.

Hero of landless campesinos in the south was Emiliano Zapata. He and Madero held several meetings in August 1911.

Some haciendas stretched over millions of acres of Mexican land. *(Courtesy of Bridgeman Art Library)*

Zapata refused to listen to Madero's argument that democracy would cure all the nation's ills. To Zapata the president's democratic idealism was a jumble of empty words. Zapata's own brother, Eufemio, told him, "This little man [Madero] has already betrayed the cause and he's too delicate to be head of the revolution. It would better to break with him: he's not going to keep any of his promises." Emiliano Zapata agreed with his brother, but took a wait-and-see attitude toward Madero in the beginning of his presidency. Nothing could change Zapata's belief that landownership was as important to the Mexican people as were breath and blood.

Emiliano Zapata was born in 1879 in the village of Anenecuilco, located in the heart of Morelos. He was of mostly Indian blood. His family was poor but respected in the village of four hundred people. His grandfather had fought in the 1810 War of Independence against Spain. When Emiliano was only nine years old, he first witnessed the power exercised by a large landholder. A hacienda owner who had close ties with the state government leveled an entire neighborhood near Anenecuilco in order to create grazing land for his horses. A local legend says Emiliano found his father weeping over the ruins of the neighborhood chapel.

"But why don't you fight?" Emiliano asked.

"Because they are powerful," his father answered.

The nine-year-old future revolutionary leader shook his head. His father was the strongest, toughest man he ever knew. Emiliano could not understand why his father and the other village men cowered under hacienda authority.

As a youth, Zapata was athletic, and the best horseman the local people had ever seen. He worked on ranches and for a while held a job as a trick rider for a rodeo show. His work took him to Mexico City, a place his neighbors thought was a foreign world. Always Zapata returned to the village, and always he saw the hacienda's property grow while the village ejido shrank. By the time Zapata was in his twenties, the local campesinos had been reduced to sharecroppers who farmed parcels of land "rented" to them by the hacienda owners.

In 1909, the villagers chose Zapata to go to the governor of Morelos and ask his help to reclaim the lands taken from them by the hacienda. The governor sent Zapata home, refusing even to talk to him. The mere request the villagers made to the governor infuriated the hacienda owner so greatly he forbade the campesinos from farming even as sharecroppers. After this incident, Zapata concluded that landowners in Morelos would never peacefully surrender their stolen ejido properties. If the campesinos wanted their ejidos back, they would have to retake them with guns, clubs, machetes, or whatever other weapons they could gather. Emiliano Zapata became a revolutionary, and he was destined to be the most honored and loved Mexican revolutionary leader during this bloody and violent era.

Under Zapata's leadership the great hacienda war began in Morelos. His method of battle was simple: attack haciendas and make off with horses, rifles, and whatever cash his men could find. In combat he was bold and inventive. Early in the campaign he commandeered a train that ran on a special track built to connect the large haciendas. Loading his men aboard the train, he sent it crashing full speed through a hacienda gate. The surprised defenders surrendered the hacienda.

The government, first under Díaz and then under the interim president de la Barra, sent armies into the south to crush

Emiliano Zapata (seated, middle) and his staff *(Library of Congress)*

the Zapatista rebellion. When the troops could not flush the Zapatistas out of the mountain region they resorted to terror tactics. Suspected Zapata supporters were not only hanged, they were hanged over a smoldering fire so they suffered the triple agonies of smoke in their lungs, fire at their feet, and rope around their necks. One general, Juvencio Robles, boasted, "If they [the Zapatistas] resist me, I shall hang them like earrings to the trees."

Despite the cruelties imposed by government soldiers, the hacienda war raged on. When Zapata took over a hacienda, he gave away portions of land to the local people and told them to farm it while at the same time protecting it from government soldiers. Often Zapata's male and female supporters tilled the soil with rifles slung around their shoulders. As the Zapata movement grew, his peasant army took over scores of haciendas as well as several small cities.

In his office in Mexico City, Madero was horrified by reports of the brutality of the hacienda war. He agreed the large haciendas should be split up and land granted to the peasants.

But President Madero insisted that hacienda owners be paid for the land they would lose. Therefore, land reform would have to wait until the Mexican treasury had sufficient money. Zapata scoffed at the need to pay the hacienda owners. He suspected the payment scheme was a delaying tactic used by Madero. He also pointed out that the haciendas had stolen land from village ejidos, and no one offered to pay the villagers.

On November 27, 1911, Zapata made a grand gesture that will be remembered forever in the pages of Mexican history. At the tiny town of Ayala in Morelos, a ragtag band played the Mexican national anthem. Emiliano Zapata, with the flag of Mexico draped around him, emerged from an adobe hut. There he revealed the Plan of Ayala, his program for land reform. The Plan said, in part,

> We declare that the land, forest and water which have been usurped by the Plantation-owners, científicos or chieftains under the cover of tyranny and venal justice shall become forthwith the property of the villages or citizens who have the appropriate deeds and have been disposed through the trickery of our oppressors. Such property will be resolutely defended with arms in hand.

The Plan of Ayala shocked landowners and other conservative, pro-business Mexicans. They thought it outrageous that a bunch of Indian farmers, led by a man who could barely read and write, could dare take over hacienda land and defend their holdings with rifles and pistols. Others worried that the traditional Indian farming methods would be incompatible with more modern business methods. Either way, it was insurrection on a grand scale, and the hacienda owners demanded that their president subdue the land thieves.

Conservative Mexico City newspapers branded President Madero a coward for his failure to stop the revolutionary uprisings. One writer claimed his vegetarian diet somehow made the president unmanly and therefore incapable of commanding the nation. Other editorial writers longed for the stability of the Diaz era. A popular Mexico City daily asked, "What remains for us of the order, peace, prosperity, and respect abroad which Mexico enjoyed under the government of General Diaz?"

Adding to Madero's problems was the American ambassador to Mexico, Henry Lane Wilson. Like many Mexican businessmen, Wilson believed Madero to be a dangerous radical. The ambassador was particularly enraged when Madero levied a tax on oil companies in order to fund public education in Mexico. At the time American firms owned huge oil fields throughout the nation. Wilson sent prejudiced and often erroneous reports to Washington about unrest in Mexico. In January 1912, he wrote that Mexico was, "seething with discontent" even though revolutionary warfare at the time was largely confined to the south. Later Wilson sent still another cable to Washington: "There is no peace, there is no order, the rabble is rising, this government cannot stand. The man [Madero] is mad."

With Madero's popularity waning and his list of enemies growing, it was not long before ambitious men sought to overthrow him and seize the presidency. The most dangerous of these would-be presidents was Pascual Orozco, an ex-mule driver and a onetime ally of Pancho Villa. In March 1912, Orozco began a rebellion in the north. The rebel leader had a well-equipped army of 6,000 men. His rifles and horses were supplied largely by the Terrazas and Creel families of northern Mexico. These two families were powerful landowners who feared that someday Madero would implement his talked-about plan for land reform.

Henry Lane Wilson, the American ambassador to Mexico *(Library of Congress)*

Pascual Orozco hoped to march his army south to Mexico City, gathering followers as he traveled. His rebellion had a bloody beginning in the northern state of Chihuahua. Orozco's men loaded a train with dynamite and sent it screaming

Pascual Orozco *(Library of Congress)*

head-on into another train carrying federal troops. Most of the government soldiers riding the train were killed in the explosion. The few survivors were too dazed to fight back against Orozco's soldiers.

Madero called upon General Victoriano Huerta to quell Orozco's rebellion. *(Library of Congress)*

To put down the Orozco uprising, Madero turned to General Victoriano Huerta. Huerta was a brutal but effective officer. During the Díaz years, he had crushed many revolts among the Indians. His fellow officers knew Huerta as a hard drinker, a drug user, and a corrupt soldier who routinely pocketed army funds.

President Madero detested war, and he had deep misgivings about the character of General Huerta. Yet the president believed he had no choice but to defeat the Orozco army by force.

After two battles in northern Mexico, Huerta routed Orozco's troops. Pascual Orozco was forced to flee across the border and take exile in Texas. The victory enhanced Huerta's prestige among fellow military men, and many gravitated to his camp.

Huerta, aware of his power, began plotting against President Francisco Madero.

FIVE

The Tragic Ten Days

Madero's Mexico teemed with generals. Leaders of even the tiniest guerrilla bands called themselves generals and sought the prestige and riches associated with that rank. From this vast pool of generals came power-hungry men eager to depose Madero and seize the presidency. One ambitious self-proclaimed general was Félix Díaz, nephew of the ex-dictator Porfirio Diaz. Félix Díaz enjoyed the support of landowners and businessmen who wished to return to the comforts they enjoyed under the regime of his famous uncle. A group of wealthy men gave Félix Díaz a large sum of money and asked him to bring back the good old days.

At two o'clock in the morning of February 9, 1913, a column of soldiers equipped with horse-drawn cannons wound their way along a lonely street that cut through Mexico City's lovely Chapultepec Park. The soldiers marched quietly, but they created enough of a racket to alert a security guard. The guard notified his superior. Word of the unusual troop

In 1913 Félix Díaz led troops toward the National Palace in Mexico City. *(Library of Congress)*

movement soon reached Gustavo Madero, the president's brother. Gustavo Madero represented the muscle behind the presidency. Unlike his brother, Gustavo believed in dealing out harsh punishments to upstart generals.

And unlike his brother, he was quick to recognize treachery. As soon as he was told of troops on the march, Gustavo hurried to the National Palace, which stood at the Zócalo.

Gustavo Madero, Francisco Madero's brother *(Library of Congress)*

The soldiers advancing in the night were part of the coup d'état hatched by General Félix Díaz and his supporters. Díaz was confident the coup d'état would be an easy operation because officers of the guard unit protecting the president were fellow conspirators and they had promised their men would put up no resistance. But Díaz did not know that Gustavo Madero had arrived at the National Palace hours earlier and replaced the disloyal officers with his own men.

It was a Sunday morning when the column of rebel troops approached Zócalo. The plaza was crowded with churchgoers headed for Mass at the towering National Cathedral that rose on the Zócalo's north side. Feeling a surge of confidence, the men crossed the plaza to the National Palace, the seat of presidential authority.

Suddenly a shot pierced the morning calm. Then a crescendo of rifle fire rang out. Machine guns appeared on the

The National Palace in Mexico City *(Library of Congress)*

roof of the National Palace and sprayed the Zócalo. The officer leading the rebels fell off his horse, dead with a bullet in his face. After ten minutes the gunfire diminished and the invading troops fled. The plaza was covered with corpses. Blood-soaked wounded people cried out in pain. Most of the dead and wounded were parishioners on their way to Mass.

What followed is known in Mexican history as the *Decena Trágica*, the Tragic Ten Days. It was a nightmare period when a pitched ten-day battle was fought in the heart of the city crowded with some 1 million people. The Mexican capital had not experienced such bloodshed since the Spaniards conquered the Aztecs four hundred years earlier.

Félix Díaz and the rebel soldiers retreated about a mile away from the Zócalo to a thick-walled building called the

Ciudadela, the Citadel. There they set up artillery and began to bombard the Zócalo area. Within minutes several downtown buildings crumbled under the impact of shells. A dozen fires broke out. Civilians ran screaming through the streets.

In the National Palace, President Madero made a strange decision. He gave command of the city to General Victoriano Huerta and told him to crush the Félix Díaz uprising. Though Madero mistrusted Huerta, he again felt he had no choice but to ask the general for help. General Huerta eagerly accepted the assignment. He lined the Zócalo with big guns and ordered his men to fire toward the Citadel. A thundering artillery duel began in the city center.

Days followed hellish nights on the urban battlefield. Entire neighborhoods were leveled. Families slept under mattresses to ward off shell splinters. Women who were

Many Mexico City citizens died in the streets during the *Decena Trágica*. *(Library of Congress)*

forced to venture into the streets to seek food held up white sheets tied to brooms. Their flags of innocence gave them no protection as the mindless cannonading raged on. Bodies littered the streets.

Even inexperienced soldiers observing this bloody scene wondered what good the cannon fire did. Gunners at the Zócalo were unable to hit the Citadel because too many tall buildings stood in their line of fire. Artillerymen at the Citadel faced the same obstacles. Yet the two generals—especially General Huerta—continued the bombardments even though they knew they were only killing civilians huddling in their homes.

Unknown to the suffering civilians, General Huerta looked upon this battle as a grand opportunity for him to become president. He despised Madero and had long planned to overthrow him. The general hoped the murderous cannonading would make the people of Mexico City demand peace at any price. If Madero was forced to step down from office, Huerta could then assume the presidency and declare peace to a relieved city. The general believed he could strike a deal with Félix Díaz. All he needed was a mediator to arrange a meeting between General Díaz and himself. Huerta found that mediator in American ambassador Henry Lane Wilson.

Wilson, a corporate lawyer from Indiana, favored "dollar diplomacy"—a belief that an American diplomat's primary mission was to advance the cause of American businesses operating abroad. In Mexico, American companies had for years made enormous profits because they employed cheap labor and paid virtually no taxes. Then Madero became president. While he did little to change the privileges American companies enjoyed, he nonetheless spoke of a future Mexico where large companies had to pay taxes and where labor unions would have the right to organize. To Wilson, such talk bordered on communism. Madero had to go.

Ambassador Wilson helped to arrange a series of secret meetings between Huerta and Félix Díaz. Gustavo Madero got wind of these meetings and demanded an explanation from General Huerta. Huerta admitted holding secret talks with Díaz but claimed his discussions were an effort to get the rebel leader to surrender. When Gustavo was unconvinced, Huerta ordered a battalion of troops to assault the Citadel in broad daylight. The troops were cut down in a withering cross fire from the Citadel's defenders. Huerta knew he was sending the attackers into certain death, but he was willing to sacrifice them in a farcical demonstration of his good intentions.

While Huerta was busy deceiving the president's brother, the cannons rained ever greater destruction on Mexico City. Stores, hospitals, churches, and apartment buildings crumbled to rubble. Fires blazed out of control. People huddled in the wreckage of their homes, too terrified to step outside. As the shells thundered, Mexico City dwellers ate pet cats and dogs in order to survive. Bodies and parts of bodies lay strewn in the street.

Battered residents feared disease would spread because of the decomposing corpses. During lulls in the shelling, volunteers rushed into the streets, pushed the bodies into piles, doused them with gasoline, and set them aflame. One witness said of these grisly bonfires, "It was a spectacle difficult to forget. When the dead were burned . . . they writhed as if they were trying to sit up."

This photo shows the destruction caused by bullets and shells during the *Decena Trágica*. *(Library of Congress)*

The Tragic Ten Days lasted from February 9 to February 18, 1913. While the capital's residents trembled under a storm of shells, Félix Díaz and Victoriano Huerta concluded a secret pact.

Historians later called the agreement the Pact of the Embassy because it had the full blessing of Ambassador Henry Lane Wilson. Under terms of the pact, Huerta agreed to dismiss his guards from the National Palace and allow the Díaz coup d'état to succeed.

Then Huerta would proclaim himself acting president until elections could be held. The elections would be arranged so that Felix Díaz would win. Huerta himself would be the military power behind the presidency. When someone asked Ambassador Wilson what would happen to Madero, he laughed and said, "Oh, Mr. Madero will be taken to an insane asylum, where he should have been all along."

On the afternoon of February 18, General Huerta was conveniently absent from the National Palace. He was instead at a hotel safely away from the shelling, having lunch with Gustavo Madero. While they dined, a team of specially trained soldiers rushed into President Madero's office and seized him and Vice President Pino Suárez. The luncheon at the hotel was interrupted by a telephone call. Huerta excused himself to answer it. The caller told him the president was under custody. Huerta reentered the dining room, a pistol in his hand. He announced to Gustavo Madero that he was under arrest.

The shelling that had spread terror in Mexico City for ten days ceased. Dazed survivors emerged from their shelters to look at the wreckage of their city. Many people fell to their knees and prayed in thanksgiving for the sudden silence. Church bells pealed. Ambassador Wilson sent a telegram to Washington: "Mexico has been saved! From now on we shall have peace, progress, and prosperity!"

The *Decena Trágica* was over. Huerta was in command of Mexico City. Now he had to decide the fate of the previous leaders. Huerta hated Gustavo Madero even more than he did the president. As soon as the shelling diminished, Huerta turned Gustavo over to a band of Díaz's men in the Citadel. Most of Díaz's followers were bandits, not soldiers, and had gotten drunk celebrating their victory. The men beat and kicked Gustavo Madero and gouged him with their bayonets. When he dropped to his knees, pleading for his life, they laughed. Finally, mercifully, an officer shot him in the head.

President Madero and Vice President Pino Suárez remained under arrest in Huerta's hands. The president had no idea his brother had been savagely murdered. The rest of the world learned of Gustavo's death the next day, when Mexico City newspapers carried the story on their front pages. Now it was clear the lives of Madero and Pino Suárez were in grave danger.

Dozens of foreign capitals, including Washington, sent urgent letters to Huerta imploring him not to harm Madero. A personal appeal came from Pedro Lascuráin, who served as Madero's foreign minister. According to Lascuráin, General Huerta tore off his shirt to expose the Virgin of Guadalupe medal he wore around his neck. The Virgin of Guadalupe is Mexico's patron saint and her image is sacred. Holding the medal near his heart, Huerta swore by the Virgin that he would not harm Madero. Lascuráin was satisfied by this oath.

Still, Madero's family feared for his life. Huerta refused to speak with Madero's wife, Sara, so she appeared before Ambassador Wilson. During a long and tearful interview, Sara expressed her dread that Huerta would soon murder her husband. She showed Wilson a letter from Madero's mother, begging the ambassador to help rescue her son. Wilson replied that Madero's fate was in the hands of General Huerta. Any move on his part to influence Huerta's decisions would amount to American intervention in Mexico's internal affairs. Wilson claimed it was not his policy to meddle in Mexico's political matters.

It was near midnight on the night of February 22, 1913, when an officer entered the room where Francisco Madero was being held. The officer said that Madero and the vice president were being transferred to a prison on the outskirts of Mexico City. Madero and Pino Suárez were put into separate cars and driven into the night. At the edge of town, the cars braked to a stop. The doors swung open, and Madero and Pino Suárez were pushed out. An officer shot them both repeatedly in the head. During the assassinations, Huerta was at the American Embassy where he and Ambassador Wilson hosted a Washington's Birthday party.

The next morning Huerta announced that Madero and Pino Suárez were shot and killed while attempting to escape custody. Ambassador Wilson sent a telegram to his superiors in Washington, urging them to accept the explanation.

SIX

Huerta

The democratic gains ushered in by Madero were quickly cast aside by Huerta. After taking office, Huerta jailed 110 members of Congress. The press was gagged again. Huerta dismissed judges, replacing them with his handpicked cronies. Félix Díaz, who now trembled under Huerta's authority, was shipped to Japan on a diplomatic mission. Elections did take place, but the vote count was unimportant. Huerta had already declared himself the winner and the new president.

The Huerta regime was harsher and more brutal than Porfirio Díaz's. To prevent a counterrevolution, Huerta had one hundred Madero supporters shot. A particularly courageous congressman named Belisario Domínguez delivered a speech condemning Huerta as a tyrant. During the speech, the congressman predicted his own assassination because he dared to criticize the president. Two weeks later Domínguez's bullet-ridden body was found in a ditch in a Mexico City suburb.

While Huerta fought with cunning and cruelty to keep his office, he showed little zest for the day-to-day work of the presidency. He enjoyed drinking cognac and smoking marijuana. He preferred barrooms and gambling houses to the presidential office. His time as president was characterized by government limousines racing from one Mexico City saloon to another as harried bureaucrats tried to find the president to have him sign vital papers.

Despite his many deficiencies, Huerta enjoyed powerful supporters. The landowners were kindly disposed toward him, as was the American business community. The army

The Mexican Catholic Church supported Huerta because he opposed limiting the powers of the church. Seen in this 1899 photo is the Cathedral of Mexico. *(Library of Congress)*

was proud that one of their own was president. And he had the blessings of the Catholic Church, an important force in the nation.

The Mexican Catholic Church had a speckled history. At the time of the Spanish Conquest, the Church was a civilizing influence. The Spanish conquistadors had the mentality of pirates and enslaved the Indians, killing them and torturing them at will. Many brave Spanish priests protected the Indians from the abuses of their countrymen. But shortly after the Conquest, the Church brought the horrors of the Spanish Inquisition to Mexico. During the Inquisition years, men and women accused of being heretics were burned at the stake in the Zócalo and in other public squares.

By the 1850s the Church was the nation's largest single landowner. It dominated education and influenced government. President Benito Juárez moved to break the power of the Church. A bloody civil war, called the War of the Reform, erupted between Church supporters and those loyal to Juárez. The Juárez forces won the War of the Reform and the power of the Mexican Catholic Church was curbed. Then the Díaz government reversed the antichurch measures taken by Juárez. Under Díaz, the Church regained much of its old power and influence.

Madero's election angered Church leaders. As president, Madero wanted to reinforce Mexico's 1857 constitution, which had been adopted by Juárez. That constitution limited Church powers in Mexico. Huerta, as was true with Díaz before him, ignored the 1857 constitution and allowed the Church to regain its old privileges. In return, priests held special masses celebrating Huerta's presidency.

Because of its support of men like Díaz and Huerta, the Catholic Church became a villain in the eyes of Mexican revolutionaries. Still, few of the revolutionary leaders proclaimed atheism. Instead they declared that the Catholic Church of Mexico had drifted away from God. Thus the Revolution embraced an anticlerical (antichurch rather than atheistic) position. Pancho Villa echoed the views of revolutionaries when he told a writer, "I do not deny belief in God. I affirm it and certify to it since it has comforted me and all men in many of life's crises. But I do not consider everything sacred that is covered by the name of religion. Most so-called religious men use religion to promote their own interests, not the things they preach . . ."

Despite Huerta's support from landowners, the Catholic Church, and the U.S. government, more and more Mexicans were turning against him. By killing Madero, Huerta had succeeded only in making him a martyr. Even those generals and politicians who thought Madero was an incompetent president now praised him and called upon Mexicans to take up arms and overthrow his murderer. One of the men intent on deposing Huerta was Venustiano Carranza, the governor of the northern state of Coahuila.

Venustiano Carranza was an unlikely revolutionary leader. Of European descent, he was born into a family of rich landowners. He enjoyed elegant food and always wore tailored suits. Pancho Villa once complained that Carranza smelled of "damned perfume" instead of sweat and dust, as Villa thought a man should smell. Carranza was a Madero supporter, and he refused to accept Huerta as president after the assassination. Calling his supporters together, he announced still another plan—the Plan of Guadalupe. The plan was simple: It

Venustiano Carranza *(Library of Congress)*

called for the overthrow of Huerta and the restoration of the 1857 constitution. With dissatisfaction with Huerta running rampant, Carranza had little trouble assembling an army. He began to call himself the First Chief of the Revolution.

Northern Mexicans always considered themselves distinctly different from their countrymen in Mexico City and the south. The north is bleak desert land, home to Indian tribes and tough, independent ranchers. The desolate region was never truly conquered by the Spaniards, nor was it ruled tightly by Mexico City. A frontier spirit prevailed in the north, breeding men such as Carranza, the First Chief; Pancho Villa, the bandit turned revolutionary; and finally the man who would become the most successful leader of the Revolution—Alvaro Obregón, from the state of Sonora.

Alvaro Obregón became a rebel leader after the assassination of President Madero. *(Library of Congress)*

Like Carranza, Obregón was of European descent. Some historians say he was Irish and his family name at one time was O'Brien. Unlike Carranza, though, he had not been born into wealth. As a young man Obregón worked as a small farmer, a mechanic in a factory, and a schoolteacher. He once invented and patented a farm implement that picked chick peas mechanically. Obregón had lived among the Yaqui Indians in Sonora, and had witnessed them being robbed of their land during the Díaz dictatorship. He sympathized with his Indian neighbors, and an alliance grew between this white man and the dispossessed and angry Yaquis. He became their general and Yaqui warriors flocked to fill his ranks. A onetime Madero supporter, Obregón became a revolutionary after the assassination.

At first Obregón's army was made up almost entirely of Yaquis armed only with bows and arrows. Despite their lack of weapons, the Yaquis fought with a desperate fury that

Obregón's army was composed almost entirely of Yaqui Indians. (*Library of Congress*)

struck terror into the hearts of their opponents. Stripped of the land they loved, the Yaqui warriors raced screaming into battle, like men who had nothing to lose.

In Mexico City, President Huerta found himself surrounded. To the south raged the hacienda war led by Emiliano Zapata. In the north Obregón assembled his force of Yaquis, while Pancho Villa gathered an army made up of unemployed mestizo mine workers. In the northwest Carranza built his army around hard-riding cowboys. The armies of the north bought their weapons from willing arms dealers in the United States. They raised money by rustling cattle and holding wealthy landowners for ransom payments.

The northern generals—Villa, Obregón, and Carranza—operated independently of one another. Not one of the three trusted the other, but they proclaimed some common goals. They were officially anticlerical, and they called for the ouster of Victoriano Huerta. The leaders of the north also said they wanted to reestablish the constitution of 1857. Carranza, Obregón, and Villa became known as the Constitutionalists. Finally all the armies had a common slogan, which they used to recruit troops and instill bravery. It was a simple saying, but it became the ringing battle cry of the Revolution: *Tierra y Libertad*! (Land and Liberty!)

To counter the strength of his enemies, Huerta mustered an army of his own. He drew his army primarily from the men of Mexico City, one of the few places in the nation where he enjoyed complete control. All males between fifteen and forty were obligated to serve. Huerta sent recruiters to the bullfights, to the saloons, anywhere men might gather. Mexico City men were afraid to walk the streets lest they be abducted and conscripted by Huerta's officers. Some men ventured outside with babies in their arms, hoping that the presence of an infant would ward off the recruiters. The tactic failed. The men were grabbed and hurried off to army barracks, leaving distraught mothers to pick up their babies at the police station. Using these strong-arm tactics, Huerta built a force of 200,000 men.

By late 1913 practically everyone in Mexico was swept up in the whirlwind force of revolution. Lawyers, doctors, and college students served in rebel armies alongside barefoot peasants. Some soldiers had clear ideas and burning convictions as to why they fought: Death to the tyrant Huerta; down with the rich; land to the campesinos. Others joined the revolution simply because they were overwhelmed with the excitement of the times. One of Villa's men told an American journalist, "It is good, fighting, you don't have to work in the mines."

Across the border, United States government leaders watched the situation in Mexico with growing concern. Shortly after Madero's assassination the ex-college professor Woodrow Wilson was inaugurated as president. Wilson rejected dollar diplomacy. He had become an admirer of Madero and hoped to see a democratic government rise in Mexico. The new president recalled Ambassador Henry Lane Wilson (no relation) from Mexico, because he suspected the ambassador had given false reports to former president Taft. But although Woodrow Wilson was well-meaning, he became in many ways another meddling American politician. Wilson harbored a belief that Latin American people needed the guidance from their more sophisticated neighbors in the north in order to form solid governments. "I am going to teach the South American republics how to elect good men," he once said.

President Woodrow Wilson believed Mexico needed political guidance from the U.S. *(Library of Congress)*

Wilson sent his representative, John Lind, a former governor of Minnesota, to investigate the turmoil in Mexico. Lind did not speak Spanish and he knew little about Mexican culture or history. From the beginning of his mission, Lind clashed with Huerta and urged President Wilson to support Carranza. Heeding Lind's advice, Wilson allowed American arms dealers to sell weapons to the Constitutionalists, but he forbade such sales to Huerta's federal army. When the arms embargo failed to break Huerta's grip on the country, Wilson sought an excuse to invade the land south of the border.

John Lind, U.S. ambassador to Mexico under President Wilson *(Library of Congress)*

Lind's Report

John Lind sympathized with the plight of Mexico's workers. In 1914 Lind toured a sugar plantation near Veracruz. He was shocked by the working conditions and was particularly upset by the fact that the plantation was owned by an American. Lind reported: "I saw an uncommon sight for the twentieth century: groups of eight to ten men scattered throughout the plantation were accompanied by an overseer . . . with a pair of pistols in his belt and an eight-to-ten foot whip in his hand . . . I [was] astounded that such a situation could exist, but it did."

In the Gulf of Mexico port of Tampico, an American warship docked to take on supplies. The ship was on a routine mission. A small group of American sailors on shore leave wandered by mistake into a restricted area. They were arrested. After several hours the Americans were released. The Tampico chief of police apologized to the American captain, saying the whole affair had been a mistake. But the American captain would not accept a mere apology. He demanded a twenty-one-gun salute to insure that Mexicans forever afterward respected the American flag. The Tampico chief of police refused on the grounds that giving such a salute would be a blow to Mexican pride.

The Tampico incident gave President Wilson the pretext he needed. As the sun rose on April 21, 1914, U.S. Marines climbed from their ships and took possession of the port of Veracruz. At first the occupation was peaceful. Then, in the

This photo shows Veracruz's Naval Institute after it was damaged by shells from a U.S. warship. *(Library of Congress)*

afternoon, a group of cadets at Veracruz's Naval Institute took it upon themselves to defend Mexican soil from the hated Yankee invaders. The cadets attacked the Marines, and a wild gunfight broke out. The Marines were supported by warships, whose heavy guns shelled the city. When the gunfire abated, more than three hundred Mexicans lay dead. Most were civilians. American casualties were slight.

In Mexico City a furious Huerta stormed and raged over the American action. He threatened to launch a bizarre plan: to attack Texas, march across the southern states, and then arm southern blacks and rally them into rebellion. Certainly Huerta's threats were hollow, but the American occupation of Veracruz served to strengthen his hand at home. No Mexican ever forgave or forgot the disastrous war of 1846-1848, which gave the United States California, Texas, and other territory that had once belonged to Mexico. Now the bully to the north had again struck Mexican soil. Mexican patriots, even those who despised Huerta, rallied behind him when he denounced the invasion.

The American navy and the Marines occupied Veracruz for seven months. During that time Mexico City mobs broke the windows of American-owned buildings and toppled the statue of George Washington that stood downtown. The American flag was burned on the streets. American businessmen and tourists were attacked by angry men and women.

The outrage felt over the invasion of Veracruz could not save Huerta's skin. From Zapata's peasant army in the south to the Constitutionalist uprising in the north, the vise was closing.

SEVEN

War Consumes Mexico

"For me the war began when I was born," said Pancho Villa. "God brought me into the world to battle." Few people had reason to doubt the guerrilla leader's statement. As war became a way of life, Villa's army emerged as the most daring and the most feared of the revolutionary bands that ravaged the north. Pancho Villa was a bandit. He claimed he was forced into that underground profession because of a tragic boyhood. A dark-skinned mestizo, he grew up in the northern state of Durango, where his father was an impoverished sharecropper. He became an outlaw after he shot and killed a wealthy landowner. The landowner, according to a story often told by Villa, had raped his sister.

Forced to go on the run, Villa joined a gang of cattle rustlers. To celebrate his membership in the gang, he changed his name from Doroteo Arango (the name given to him at birth) to Francisco (Pancho) Villa. He chose the name Pancho Villa to honor a local bandit chief who had just been killed.

Mexicans distinguish between bandidos (bandits) and ladrónes (thieves). A ladrón steals from his friends and his neighbors, and is considered despicable. A bandido, on the other hand, is a bit of a Robin Hood. Bandidos rob from the people who already have far more than they need. The true bandido uses his money to help the poor. During the harsh years of revolutionary fighting, Villa often gave away food supplies

Pancho Villa as a young boy

to impoverished villagers. However, when he doled out food, he made certain there was a journalist or two present to record the event. Villa was protective of his image, and he enjoyed promoting his reputation as a man of the people.

A lifetime of experience as a bandit gave Pancho Villa the skills he needed to wage what he felt was a holy war against Huerta and his army. His first major victory came at the border town of Ciudad Juárez, a city he had captured three years earlier for his hero Madero. At the second battle of Ciudad Juárez, Villa's army was small. Villa knew a cavalry charge against the Juárez garrison would be suicidal. So he and his men commandeered a train pulling hopper cars filled with coal. They dumped the coal and climbed into the cars, using the train as both a Trojan Horse and as an armored personnel carrier. When the fedcral troops at Ciudad Juárez saw the engine and the long string of cars approach, they were not alarmed—it seemed to be just another coal train. Then, as the train neared the federal army's position, Villa's men popped up firing their rifles from the protection of the thick-walled iron cars. Ciudad Juárez fell to Villa, and the federals suffered major casualties.

Villa's cavalry charges became the stuff of legends. His men were called dorados, the golden ones, so named for their gold-hued uniforms. The Dorados wore broad cartwheel hats and often had bandolcers of ammunition slung crosswise over their chests. Their general, Pancho Villa, led every cavalry charge himself. Above the thunder of hoof beats the Dorados rode their horses into battle, shrieking: "Viva Villa! Viva la Revolución!"

During the course of the Revolution, Villa's cavalry charges became legendary. *(Courtesy of AP Images)*

Villa stood six feet tall and weighed a muscular two hundred pounds. On foot he walked with a clumsy gait, stumbling often. But on horseback he displayed the grace of an Olympian. His face was a mask of anger when he led a charge. To him fear was a disease that plagued lesser men.

The American journalist John Reed met Villa in 1913 and was taken in by his fierce looks: "He is the most natural human being I ever saw, natural in the sense of being nearest to a wild animal. He says almost nothing . . . If he isn't smiling he's looking gentle. All except his eyes, which are never still and full of energy and brutality. They are as intelligent as hell and as merciless . . . They're like a wolf's."

Because they had to cover great distances, the armies of the north traveled on trains. Villa's troop movements resembled mass migrations. Horses rode on cattle cars, artillery on flatcars, soldiers on boxcars, and officers in the caboose. The trains were always overcrowded, and younger soldiers were assigned to sit on the roofs of boxcars.

American journalist John Reed reported on the Mexican Revolution by following Villa's army. *(Library of Congress)*

Mexican revolutionaries relied on trains for troop transportation.
(Library of Congress)

The federal army also relied on trains to transport its soldiers. Consequently, northern Mexico's railroad lines became long, narrow battlefields. Hand-pumped cars or old engines were loaded with dynamite and used as torpedoes to destroy enemy trains. Retreating armies tore up tracks to frustrate their pursuers. Track laying engineers and locomotive mechanics became as vital to the armies of the north as were horse soldiers.

In the northwest, Alvaro Obregón and his Yaqui soldiers battled the federal troops. Obregón, a science buff and an inventor, waged war in a starkly different manner from the hard-driving Pancho Villa. Before taking a town or a fortified hacienda, Obregón observed the terrain, captured the high ground overlooking his objective, and determined the best approach for his attacking soldiers. An avid reader, Obregón was familiar with the techniques used by history's

In battle, Obregón employed tactics he had learned from reading about famous military leaders like Napoleon.

greatest commanders—Alexander the Great, Julius Caesar, and Napoleon. On the plains of northern Mexico, he deployed his troops with the skill of a master chess player.

As war spread over the land, successful armies grew in numbers, weapons, and strength. Guerrilla units from the hinterlands attached themselves to the best of the rebel divisions. Consequently, Obregón's became one of the most powerful armies in Mexico. The core of his soldiers remained the Yaqui Indians. They were grim men, filled with hatred for Huerta, the federal troops, and for rich people in general.

The Yaqui infantry fought as if death held little meaning to them. Guided by Obregón's brilliant tactics, the Yaquis and other troops were molded into an almost unbeatable army.

In theory, both Obregón and Villa were under the command of Venustiano Carranza, the self-proclaimed First Chief of the Revolution. Many of the orders issued by the First Chief, however, were ignored by the other two northern generals.

Carranza had little appetite for war and hated field conditions. He traveled in a private three-car train with his private chef serving regular meals. In his early fifties, he was considered to be an old man by his fellow revolutionaries, and he had a frustrating inability to make up his mind during a crisis. When asked for his views on a crucial matter, Carranza would comb his long white beard and then simply shrug his shoulders. Pancho Villa delighted in calling the First Chief "Old Goat Whiskers." A politician rather than a warrior, Carranza longed to arrive in Mexico City, where the seat of governmental power lay.

To the south, the Zapatistas were more an insurgent people than they were an army. Rarely did they fight battles on well-defined fronts. Instead the Zapatistas staged surprise raids against haciendas and small towns. When overwhelmed by federal troops, they cast aside their rifles and blended into the surroundings by becoming simple country people.

As long as they held on to their land, the Zapatistas were unconcerned about who was in power in Mexico City. They were driven only by a desire to retake the ejidos seized by hacienda owners. Zapata inspired his men with simple, direct statements: "Men of the south! It is better to die on your feet than to live on your knees!"

Zapata and Communism

Because Zapata was so passionate about land reform, newspapers in the United States began accusing him of being a Communist. Taking land from rich people and giving it to poor farmers was a program of the Communist Party in various parts of the world during the early 1900s. Zapata, who had a very limited education, in fact knew nothing about communism, as this interview with the Mexican lawyer Sota y Gamma suggests:

"Emiliano, what do you think of communism?"
"Explain to me what it is."
"For example, all the people of a village farm [harvest] their lands together and then they distribute the harvest equally."
"Who makes the distribution?"
"A representative or council elected by the community."
"Well look, as far as I'm concerned, if any "somebody"
. . . would try to distribute the fruits of my labor . . . I would fill him with bullets."

The federal army suffered defeat after defeat against the rebel forces, both in the north and in the south. The federal soldiers, most of whom were snatched off the streets of Mexico City and forced to serve, deserted by the thousands. As the army dissolved, the government in the Mexico City area ceased to function. Taxes went uncollected. Services came to a halt. What little law remained in Mexico gave way to anarchy.

Huerta was rarely seen in the presidential office. Instead he sat in one of his favorite downtown saloons, brooding over glasses of cognac. Edith O'Shaughnessy, the wife of an

American diplomat who lived in Mexico City, wrote, "The task of peace seems well nigh hopeless. Huerta has very little natural regard for human life. This isn't a specialty of dictators anyway."

By early 1914 three-quarters of Mexico was in rebel hands. Huerta controlled only central Mexico and the Mexico City region. Turmoil reigned in the lands occupied by revolutionary forces. Revolutionaries opened jails and invited prisoners to join their ranks. Some prisoners served as soldiers, but hardened criminals used their newfound freedom to terrorize the countryside. As war raged over the land, mines went unattended, cattle were left to roam, and weeds overwhelmed corn patches. Family life splintered as men between fourteen and seventy went off to fight. And the role of women in Mexican society underwent profound changes.

Prerevolutionary Mexican women were mothers and homemakers—little else. Even upper-class women went to school only long enough to learn basic reading and writing. Few professions were open to women. Laws forbade women from voting and restricted their right to own property. Mexico was a man's world where women were regarded largely as servants.

Then the demands of the Revolution allowed Mexican women to gain new respect. The changes came gradually and were inspired by the lowly camp followers who traditionally traveled with Mexican armies. For generations, women followers had attached themselves to Mexican soldiers. They foraged for food, cooked, and slept with the men. Often they had a baby strapped to their backs, but rarely were they married to the man they served.

At the beginning of the Revolution, camp followers attached to the Constitutionalist (northern) armies traded for food and other goods with camp followers who had assigned themselves to the federal units. In the heat of combat, the camp followers on all sides found a new role. When their man fell from a bullet or shell splinter, the woman simply picked up his rifle and took his place on the battle line. If they survived the battle, many of the

Women fought with the revolutionaries.

camp followers never returned to their old positions of servitude. Instead they became soldaderas, women soldiers. Shorthanded revolutionary commanders hardly cared if a woman served in the ranks alongside the men. Gradually the soldaderas assumed posts of leadership in the rebel armies. Every unit had a woman captain or major who led men into combat.

The Mexican philosopher Octavio Paz once called the uprising against Huerta a "fiesta of bullets." And at times the war took on a strange, festive atmosphere. Army camps were full of song. A traveler could recognize the armies by the songs they favored. Villistas sang "Adelita," a spirited ballad about a girl who: *además de ser valiente era bonita* (besides being brave was beautiful). Carranza's troops favored "La Cucaracha," about a cockroach that did not know where it was going. One verse of "La Cucaracha" poked fun at the slightly overweight rival general, Pancho Villa:

> *Una cosa me da risa,* (One thing makes me laugh,)
> *Pancho Villa sin camisa.* (Pancho Villa without his shirt.)

Despite the festive music, the fighting was brutal and merciless, the violence an outgrowth of the era of injustice and oppression leading up to the war. Years of the rich exploiting the poor and the whites lording over the nonwhites planted seeds of hatred that blossomed into terrible wartime atrocities. The shooting of prisoners became a routine practice for all sides. At one point the Villistas were short of bullets, so they ordered their prisoners to stand in tight lines of three,

In this photo taken by the Mutual Film Corporation, Villa (middle, in uniform) stands with other revolutionary leaders. *(Library of Congress)*

one behind the other. That way one bullet fired through the chest of the first man killed all three. Months later Villa had plenty of ammunition, so he told one of his lieutenants, a particularly brutal man named Rodolfo Fierro, to murder three hundred captives with his pistol. Fierro did as he was ordered and later complained that his trigger finger developed a blister.

In the south the Zapatistas dealt savagely with hacienda owners. Some owners were nailed to the door of their manor house and left there to die. Other owners and hacienda foremen were staked over anthills to be eaten alive by the swarming insects.

Moving relentlessly southward, Pancho Villa's army was the Revolution's iron fist. Blocking Villa's advance

Federal troops at Torreón *(Library of Congress)*

was the city of Torreón, a vital railroad center defended by Huerta's best troops. In the battle for Torreón, all men fought to the death because they knew prisoners were usually shot. Villa later said, "In the bloody struggle we could not break their resistance, and they could not throw us back. Cannon and machine guns seemed to come into existence in their defense, but neither their grenades nor their bullets stopped us."

After countless casualties on both sides, Torreón finally fell to Villa. Nearer to Mexico City stood the ancient silver-mining town of Zacatecas, one of the last bastions of Huerta's strength. With pistol in hand, Villa led his Dorados up sheer mountain cliffs and into the face of deadly rifle fire. Through raw courage and incredible force of will, Villa shot his way into the streets of Zacatecas. The federal soldiers, overwhelmed by this fanatical warrior, ran in panic.

Villa, the bandit-turned-rebel, became a folk hero in the United States. American newspaper reporters followed his campaign and gave eyewitness accounts of the battles. Villa was portrayed as a dashing peasant leader on a noble crusade to uplift the masses and punish the Mexican rich who had for so long treated the workers like slaves. One of the most popular of these American journalists was John Reed, who rode with Villa for four months.

American newspaper writers called Villa "Mexico's Robin Hood." An American company, the Mutual Film Corporation, paid Villa $25,000 for rights to make a movie of Villa's exploits, starring the general himself. Villa, ever searching for publicity, agreed to go into battle when there was plenty of daylight for the camera crews to capture the action. In the film he was portrayed as a hero, similar to the courageous

John Reed (1887–1920)

Born in Portland, Oregon, John Reed was educated at Harvard and became an influential newspaper and magazine reporter. In 1914 *Metropolitan Magazine* sent Reed to Mexico where he covered the revolution by following Villa's army. Largely through his writing Pancho Villa rose to the status of folk hero in the United States. Reed's book *Insurgent Mexico* told of his experiences in revolutionary Mexico and was widely read. Reed also covered the Russian revolution. In 1920 he published his most famous book, *Ten Days That Shook The World*, about the Communist uprising in Russia. Reed died of typhus in Moscow in 1920. He was given a state funeral by the Russian government and was buried in the Kremlin, the only American given that honor. The 1981 movie *Reds* tells the story of Reed's life.

men of the American West. The moviemakers overlooked Villa's habits of executing prisoners or shooting anyone who offended him in the smallest way. The movie, *The Life of General Villa*, opened in New York in May 1914.

After taking Zacatecas, Villa's army had swelled to 22,000 soldiers and soldaderas. This huge force was now poised to strike Mexico City. But Venustiano Carranza, the First Chief, considered Mexico City to be his prize. Under no circumstances would he allow Villa to steal his glory and enter the capital first. Carranza's army controlled the railroads linking Zacatecas with vital coal deposits. So Carranza stopped Villa's advance on Mexico City by ordering a halt to his coal deliveries. Without coal, Villa's trains could not run. Villa fumed and swore revenge on Carranza for this treacherous act.

In Mexico City, President Huerta packed his belongings and no doubt counted his money too. During his sixteen-month tenure in office, millions of pesos in the national treasury had mysteriously disappeared. Facing a hopeless military situation, Huerta resigned as president in July 1914. Quietly he slipped out of Mexico and took a ship to Cuba. Later he traveled to the United States. He died in Texas in 1916 of cirrhosis of the liver, a disease often brought about by alcoholism.

With Huerta gone, the people of Mexico City now waited, fearful of their fate. Who would occupy the capital? Would it be Pancho Villa, whose Dorados were known to rape women and carry off rich men for ransom? Or would the occupiers be Obregón and his Yaqui Indians? While the Mexico City dwellers worried, the people of the countryside rejoiced. Huerta, the despised dictator, was overthrown. The Constitutionalists had triumphed. At last the war, with all its violence and bloodletting, had come to an end. But victory celebrations proved to be premature. The war now had an energy of its own, and it showed no signs of ending.

EIGHT

General Versus General

In mid-August 1914, Alvaro Obregón and his fierce Yaqui soldiers marched into Mexico City. The capital's middle class stayed at home behind locked doors, terrified because they believed Obregón's men were wanton murderers. Their fears proved to be baseless. Obregón, a man who believed in strict adherence to rules, declared the city to be under martial law and announced he would shoot all looters. The general from the north brought order to a city that had been in the grip of lawlessness since the last days of Huerta.

Obregón, however, had no love for Mexico City residents. He considered the men of Mexico City to be weaklings who cowered under the dictatorship of Huerta and let their country cousins do all the fighting. "It was inexcusable for you men to have abstained from taking up arms," Obregón told a Mexico City crowd that had gathered to pay homage to the slain president, Francisco Madero. Obregón then made a dramatic gesture that would live forever in the lore of the

Revolution. Before an audience composed mainly of men, he gave his pistol to a young lady, a schoolteacher named María Arias, who had been a guerrilla fighter against the Huerta regime. "Since I know how to admire valor," Obregón said, "I cede my gun to this lady, the only person among you worthy to possess it." Forever afterward, María Arias was known as María Pistola (María Pistol) and became a genuine heroine of the Revolution.

Obregón (left, seated) poses with members of his Yaqui staff. *(Library of Congress)*

Venustiano Carranza arrived in Mexico City shortly after Obregón. The First Chief now claimed political leadership of the nation, which had been his goal since joining the conflict. In order to legitimatize his rule, Carranza ordered a convention to meet in the city of Aguas Calientes. The convention was to decide the future of Mexican government. All the revolutionary leaders were invited. Carranza was confident he could dictate the terms of the convention, but his plans fell through when delegates loyal to Villa and Zapata took charge of the meetings. They demanded radical land redistribution along the lines of Zapata's Plan of Ayala. Carranza, hesitant about land reform, ordered his delegates to leave. Sensing the coming of a war between the generals, Carranza and Obregón hastily fled Mexico City to take refuge in Veracruz. Once more the capital was an open, unguarded city.

This painting by José Clemente Orozco depicts marching Zapatistas. *(Courtesy of The Museum of Modern Art/SCALA/Art Resource)*

From the south came the Zapatistas, and from the north the Villistas swooped down upon the city of Mexico. Once more city residents waited, trembling in fear. Most of their dread was directed at the Zapatistas. The city-bred people considered Zapata's soldiers to be ignorant country brutes. Worse yet, the Zapata movement was made up of dark-skinned Indians led by a mostly Indian general. Since the time of the Spanish Conquest, the Mexico City elite had lived in fear of Indian uprisings. Now, an Indian upheaval was at their doorstep.

The Zapatistas came not in military formation, but walking in small groups. They wore white cotton clothes, the uniform of the humble field hand. It was impossible to distinguish officers from men, or even soldiers from soldaderas. Many of the Zapatistas carried banners showing pictures of the Virgin of Guadalupe, and they made the sign of the cross whenever they passed a church. All seemed awed by the towering buildings, the goods displayed in store windows, and the handsome statues that stood on the Paseo de la Reforma. Most important, their behavior was near perfect. When the markets closed, the Zapatistas knocked on doors and asked for—not demanded—food.

In early December 1914 the Villistas came to Mexico City, riding on boxcars peppered with bullet holes. At first the Villistas behaved well enough, but several of the men looted liquor stores, got drunk, and fired their rifles wildly in the air.

Zapata and Villa met for the first time in a Mexico City suburb. Although they shared similar goals, the two famous generals seemed uncomfortable in each other's presence. When they toured the National Palace, Villa sat in the president's chair, the Mexican republic's equivalent to a throne. Zapata was heard to mutter that the chair ought to be taken out to the street and burned. Zapata left the capital shortly after his meeting with Villa. Most of the Zapatistas followed their general, leaving Mexico City in the hands of the Villistas.

After their initial period of orderly behavior, the Villistas went wild. They broke into stores and stole liquor and goods. Because of their leader's contempt for Catholic authority, churches were a special target for their escapades. Religious statues bedecked with gold and silver were snatched from altars. Rapes were committed in all parts of the city, even on the open streets. Men who tried to rescue women being raped were shot. No woman was safe from attack.

Pancho Villa (seated on presidential throne) and Emiliano Zapata (to his left) in the presidential chambers of the Palacio Nacional in Mexico City, 1914.

The most notorious rape that took place during the occupation was committed by Pancho Villa himself. At the luxurious Hotel Palacio, Villa took a fancy to a young receptionist and announced he would return for her later. The terrified receptionist was sent home by the hotel manager, a refined Frenchwoman. When Villa came back, he could not find the receptionist. So, he raped the Frenchwoman. The crime was reported in newspapers. It became a worldwide scandal and forever stained the reputation of the onetime hero.

Villa and his troops soon drifted out of Mexico City, and Carranza and Obregón reoccupied the capital.

The Mexican Revolution entered a crippling, demoralizing stage that saw generals fight each other. They fought not only for their visions as to the form of government Mexico should have, but also for personal gain. Carranza, Obregón, and Villa were called Constitutionalists because they wished to install a new Constitution to guide the country. But each of the three men had aspirations to become president and waged war for that office as well as for their political beliefs. Zapata, who believed with all his heart in land reform, had little desire for a high office in postrevolutionary government. In the months and years to come, Villa fought Obregón, Carranza fought Zapata, and finally Obregón fought Carranza. Dozens of lesser generals engaged in similar fratricidal wars. Mexico's agony continued without respite.

Combat during the wars between the generals was as ferocious as it had been in the past, but the spirit of revolution evaded the common soldier. Gone was the idealism that sent armies marching to the field to avenge Madero and topple the dictator Huerta. Men still uttered the battle cry "Land and

Liberty," but the words now seemed empty. Soldiers fought for generals, not for causes.

The war sped on, driven by its own momentum like a boulder rolling downhill. Mexicans continued to kill one another, but no soldier could adequately explain the reason for the carnage. A character from *The Underdogs*, a famous novel written by a veteran of the Revolution, asks, "What I can't get into my head is why we keep on fighting. Didn't we finish off this man Huerta and his federation?"

The nation splintered into territories controlled by various generals. Within the territories the generals were the only law. They issued their own currencies and insisted their money was the only legal tender that could be used in the area they controlled. Villa's army traveled with a printing press on its troop train and printed thousands of bills with their commander's picture boldly on the face. At least twenty-five different forms of paper money—all worthless in a rival general's territory—circulated in Mexico. Only the Zapatistas issued money of value. Zapata's followers melted down silver and made coins crudely stamped out on a hand press.

In the countryside military strongmen became the new ruling class. Though the generals uttered revolutionary statements, they made life as miserable for the campesinos as did the property owners of previous years. Wherever the armies traveled, they stripped the land bare of produce and livestock. Many farmers simply gave up their crops. They hoarded enough corn to feed their families but let their fields go to weeds. Men and women were forced to join the marauding armies in order to get something to eat.

The year 1915, when the war between the generals began, was known as the Year of Hunger in Mexico City. With farm production down and various generals in control of the railroads, few food shipments reached the capital. Respectable people were forced to forage in garbage cans, searching for morsels to eat. Boys and girls who had once been well-dressed and well-fed became beggars and petty thieves. Women of all ages turned to prostitution to obtain the price of a few tortillas. Bodies of people who died in the streets from starvation and disease were picked up by death wagons and taken to mass graves outside the city. The death wagons were among the few government services that still functioned.

Villa, Zapata, Carranza, and Obregón continued their fight. Of the four, only Zapata had no desire to become president of Mexico. Villa was a field commander, and the art of political leadership escaped him. Obregón had his eye on the president's chair, but he was willing to wait for his opportunity. This left Carranza at the top of a very shaky ladder.

The most serious threat facing Carranza was Pancho Villa, who commanded a large and well-equipped army. Against Villa, Carranza could counter with Obregón and his highly disciplined Yaqui troops. Carranza and Obregón remained allies, though neither man liked or trusted the other. Obregón agreed to go to the field and destroy the army of Pancho Villa. The stage was set for the bloodiest battle of the Mexican Revolution.

Villa seemed to have all the advantages in the coming fight. His army outnumbered Obregón's by at least three to one. However, Obregón was a brilliant strategist and he understood the contrasting moods of his rival general. Villa, he believed, was in a foul mood and could be coaxed into battle on unfavorable terms. Also, Obregón had studied reports written by commanders fighting in the trenches of Europe during their

Obregón had studied reports on World War I trench warfare prior to his battle with Villa in Celaya. *(Library of Congress)*

service in World War I. The reports spelled out that modern machine guns capable of firing six hundred bullets a minute were instruments that killed on a ghastly scale.

Near the colonial town of Celaya, Obregón ordered his men to dig trenches. In front of the trenches he ran coils of barbed wire. At regular intervals he placed batteries of his newest machine guns. Obregón thus transformed the Mexican corn patches into a likeness of a World War I battlefield.

Celaya is a little more than one hundred miles north of Mexico City. A better tactician than Villa would have lured his opponent farther north to stretch out his supply lines. Villa, however, was eager to attack—as Obregón hoped he would be.

With bugles blaring and cries of "Viva Villa!" the battle of Celaya began on April 6, 1915. Following his foremost military instinct—charge!—Villa led some 30,000 cavalry and

As Villa charged Obregón's trenches, his troops were mowed down by machine gunfire. *(Courtesy of Library of Congress)*

foot soldiers racing toward Obregón's entrenched infantry. The result was a massacre. Obregón's machine guns blazed in carefully prepared crisscross lines of fire. The attackers who survived the deadly rain of machine gun bullets became entangled in barbed wire. Horses and men screamed in terror and agony. Inside the trenches lay Obregón's fearless Yaqui riflemen. Yaqui wives, girlfriends, and children also occupied the trenches, where they busily reloaded rifles. When a Yaqui man fell victim to a Villista bullet, the woman picked up the rifle. When she fell, the rifle was passed to the oldest boy.

The battle of Celaya lasted three days. Villa fought in the same manner that made him the feared Dorado of the north. Again and again he charged Obregón's trenches. But his fury was no match against the cool mind of Obregón and the determination of the Yaqui defenders. Four thousand Villistas were killed at Celaya and 6,000 were taken prisoner.

The Villistas retreated and the two revolutionary divisions clashed again, this time at the nearby city of León. The battle of León was another Obregón victory, but the commander was wounded when an exploding shell tore off his right arm. Obregón was in such maddening pain that he drew his pistol, pointed it at his heart, and pulled the trigger—hoping that death would end his agony. The gun did not fire, and quick medical attention saved his life.

Villa withdrew to northern Mexico. There, in his familiar mountains, his army was invincible. But his days as a chief over a large northern force were over. Never again would Pancho Villa ride at the head of the feared Dorados and act as a major power in revolutionary Mexico. In Mexico City, Carranza was delighted with Villa's defeat. Carranza now shifted his attention to the south. He still had to deal with Zapata and his stubborn peasant army.

During 1915, while the generals of the north battled one another, the Zapatistas organized a separate society in the south. In effect, they declared Morelos and their southern territory to be independent from the rest of Mexico. Under the guidelines of the Plan of Ayala, the great haciendas of the south were broken up and local people were given land. In addition to their land program, the Zapatistas ran sugar mills and operated an arms factory that refurbished old rifles.

With the intent of crushing Zapata's country-within-a-country, Carranza sent General Pablo González to the south. González was an ambitious man who also thirsted to be president. So far, however, he had failed miserably in combat. González was called The General Who Never Won A Battle, and the nickname was all too appropriate. But what González lacked in generalship he overcame in cruelty and treachery.

Upon arriving in Morelos, General González launched a campaign designed to starve out the Zapatistas. He burned crops, shot cattle, and blew up bridges used

General Pablo Gonzalez was known as The General Who Never Won A Battle. *(Library of Congress)*

by farmers. Employing terror tactics, he hanged hundreds of campesinos suspected to be Zapata sympathizers. Yet he had no success at stopping the Zapatista campesino rebellion. Although González managed to retake the cities, the countryside belonged to the white-clad peasants who worshiped Zapata as if he were a saint. Surrounded by these dedicated people, Emiliano Zapata was untouchable.

The war between the generals distressed American president Woodrow Wilson. American corporations owned more than $1 billion worth of property and machinery in Mexico. Continued warfare meant that American oil wells were not pumping and that American cattle ranches were being raided by warring bands. Businessmen urged the president to send the United States army to Mexico to stop the war and protect American interests.

Wilson tried to end the war between the generals by throwing his support behind the one man who seemed to be in the strongest position to win—Carranza. In the summer of 1915 President Wilson announced the United States would recognize Carranza as the legitimate president of Mexico. He forbade American arms merchants from selling weapons to any of Carranza's rival generals. Wilson's support of Carranza infuriated Pancho Villa, who believed the American president had stabbed him in the back. He swore revenge.

In March 1916, under the cover of darkness, Pancho Villa led 485 horsemen across the American border. Villa headed toward the town of Columbus, New Mexico. He was determined to raid an American city for two reasons: First, he wanted to punish the Americans, especially President Wilson; second, he hoped to embarrass the Carranza government. At dawn, Villa and his followers stormed down Columbus's main street, whooping, yelling, and firing wildly. Sixteen Americans were killed during the assault. The American public was outraged. Villa—once a hero in the eyes of many Americans—had killed United States citizens on American soil. The people cried out for vengeance.

President Wilson sent a force of 6,000 soldiers into Mexico to capture Villa alive or dead. The unit was led by General John Pershing, the nation's foremost cavalry commander. In Mexico City an angry President Carranza denounced the border crossing as an invasion, but there was little he could do

General John Pershing *(Library of Congress)*

to block the U.S. Army. Pershing had no luck at all in finding the elusive Villa. Even with the assistance of airplanes, which had never been seen before in the skies over northern Mexico, Villa still escaped his pursuers. Villa, the onetime highway bandit, bragged, "No one can follow me on horseback or on foot, nor on the plains nor in the mountains . . . [I'm] just like the wolves." All over the country Mexicans delighted in the Americans' inability to capture Villa. In Mexico City Carranza's strong opposition against the U.S. government strengthened support for his administration.

General Pershing withdrew from Mexico in January 1917, after chasing Villa for ten frustrating months. Mexicans rejoiced at the utter defeat of the American troops. A song, written at the time, became popular throughout the land:

> Did the Americans think
> That war was a ballroom dance?
> Back to their land they went
> With shame writ all o'er their face.

President Wilson recalled the army primarily because he believed Pershing and his men would soon be sent overseas to fight against Germany. A telegram sent by the German foreign secretary, Arthur Zimmermann, to the Carranza government had recently been intercepted by the British government. Although the note was written by a low German official, it had serious portents in the United States.

The Zimmermann telegram urged Mexico to attack its northern neighbor. Zimmermann suggested that a successful attack on the U.S. would allow Mexico to regain the territory it lost in the 1848 war, including the American states of Texas, New Mexico, and Arizona. The note did not have the backing of the German government. In fact, it was little more than a harebrained scheme dreamed up by Secretary Zimmermann.

Still, the Zimmermann telegram caused sensational headlines when the British handed it over to American authorities. Five weeks later, the United States declared war on Germany. Submarine warfare waged by the Germans was the main reason which drove the American people into the

Arthur Zimmerman

war, but certainly the Zimmerman telegram was an important factor.

As 1916 came to a close, the war between the generals still smoldered, but Mexico was exhausted after years of bloodshed. The generals, sensing that an uneasy peace was beginning to take hold of the land, scrambled to consolidate their powers. No one was yet ready to sacrifice their dream of a new Mexico, and they were still ready to fight for what they wanted.

Warring Generals

Although it could seem that the violence during this time was merely an arbitrary power grab by competing generals, this would not be an accurate view. Villa and Zapata were called the Conventionists because they were fighting to uphold the decisions reached by delegates of the Convention of Aguascalientes. Those decisions would have favored their revolutionary platforms of land reform, workers' rights, and curbing poverty. Carranza and Obregón became the Constitutionalists (although Obregón was motivated by a very different ideology, more reformist, and he allied with Carranza as a way to consolidate power).

Constitutionalists rejected the Convention of Aguascalientes because it departed too much from the Constitution of 1857. Aguascalientes is the beginning of this period of violence and what seems like several years of unchecked bloodshed purely for personal gain. But there were also fundamental ideological differences at the heart of the conflict.

NINE

Twilight of the Generals

By early 1917 the fighting in Mexico slowed, and politically, an uneasy peace settled over Mexico City. Carranza emerged, at least temporarily, as the winner in the war between the generals. Villa had been reduced to a life of banditry in northern Mexico. Zapata's peasant rebellion remained in force, but the Zapatistas were unlikely to march to the capital and overthrow the president.

Obregón was Carranza's only serious rival, and he waited his chance to seize national leadership. Some five hundred lesser generals still commanded armies. Carranza began pacifying the minor generals in a time honored fashion: by paying them off. Some generals were given huge ranches and land holdings, while others were awarded lucrative jobs in national or state government. The reforms promised by the Revolution—land and justice—were ignored by Carranza as he distributed the spoils of the nation to military strongmen.

After gaining control of Mexico in 1917, General Carranza called for a constitutional convention to draft a new constitution.

Carranza was determined to deliver on one promise. He and the other generals of the north had fought as Constitutionalists. At first they backed the Constitution of 1857. Later they claimed their primary goal in waging revolutionary war was to give the nation a new constitution to serve as the framework for a more enlightened government.

Carranza called for a constitutional convention to meet at the city of Querétaro. Villa and Zapata supporters were not invited. This time Carranza was confident he could dictate the terms of the convention. He favored a rewritten version of the 1857 constitution. Carranza instructed his delegates to steer clear of the land redistribution issue. He and most of his friends were property owners who had no desire to see their haciendas and ranches swallowed up by landless peasants. But as was true with the previous convention in Aguascalientes, the Queretaro meeting soon slipped out of Carranza's control.

The constitution writers who met in Querétaro in December 1916 were middle-class men: teachers, lawyers, and shop-keepers. They were not radicals who demanded the immediate confiscation of property belonging to the rich. Still, they had a conscience and they perceived they were performing a solemn duty. They believed they could not offer the nation a rewritten version of a sixty-year-old constitution after the people had suffered through such terrible bloodletting. So the delegates scrapped the 1857 constitution and wrote a new charter. It turned out to be an amazing document whose principles govern the nation to this day.

The new constitution was written in six weeks and approved on February 5, 1917. In many respects it was progressive beyond a reformer's dreams. Most Mexican progressives wanted strict separation between church and state. On that issue the constitution's language was clear. Catholicism had been for centuries Mexico's national religion. The new constitution made freedom of religion the law of the land. And the reform measures did not stop with religion. Article 123 recognized the right of Mexican workers to form labor unions. Other language in the document limited the workday to eight hours, prohibited child labor, and established a minimum wage. The constitution required employers to give equal pay for equal work with no distinction between men and women. No other nation in 1917 had such far-reaching workers' rights written directly into the constitution.

The constitution also tackled the divisive issue of land redistribution—the basic cause of the Revolution. Article 27 of the Constitution of 1917 gave the government the right to redistribute land as government authorities saw fit. However this article also meant that a government like Carranza's, which favored the hacienda owners, could drag its feet on land reform. Another clause said, "The lands and waters within Mexico's national territory originally belong to the nation." This was interpreted to mean the wealth of the subsoil—the minerals and oil—may be used only by Mexicans or by foreigners willing to obey all Mexican laws. The clause put severe restrictions on foreign companies that owned oil wells and silver mines in Mexico. It reflected the "Mexico For The Mexicans" mood that was prevalent throughout the Revolution.

Many world scholars, especially the liberal reformists, viewed the Mexican Constitution of 1917 as an astonishingly progressive set of laws which would guarantee the individual rights of the people in future generations. But to President Carranza the new constitution was written by radicals, and he simply ignored much of what it promised. For example, the constitution required the government to provide an education through the primary grades for all Mexican children. However, Carranza's school budget was only slightly higher than that of Porfirio Díaz's. Carranza also looked the other way at the language that forbade child labor. Many Mexican children, especially those in farming communities, continued to go to work at the age of nine or ten and never saw the inside of a classroom.

Running virtually unopposed, Carranza was elected president in March 1917. In the south the Zapatistas refused to recognize him as their leader. Addressing the president as "citizen Carranza," Zapata wrote,

> "From the time you first . . . named yourself Chief [of the Revolution], you proceeded to turn the struggle to the advantage

Despite a new constitutional requirement to provide an education for all Mexican children, Carranza's government did little to improve schools or enforce child labor laws. *(Library of Congress)*

> of yourself and the friends and allies who helped you climb and then shared the booty—riches, honors, businesses, banquets, sumptuous fiestas . . . It never entered your mind that the Revolution was for the benefit of the great masses . . . You took justice in your own hands and created a dictatorship which you gave the name 'Revolution.'"

The letter infuriated Carranza, and he ordered General Pablo González to crush the Zapatista movement once and for all. González, The General Who Never Won A Battle, stepped up his campaign and his war of terror against the campesinos. Reasoning that the Zapatistas lived off the peasants, González attempted to remove the peasants from the land. Through mass murder and forced deportation, he reduced the population of Morelos by 40 percent. Still, the campesinos that remained were willing to fight for Zapata until death. Small bands of farmers raided González's supply dumps, attacked his trains, and ambushed his troops.

Failing in his attempts to best Zapata in battle, González resorted to a desperate trick. He ordered one of his officers, a colonel named Jesús Guajardo, to approach Zapata posing as a turncoat. Through friendly farmers, Guajardo passed the word that he was anxious to switch sides and join the rebels with all his men and their weapons. Such defections were common in revolutionary Mexico. To demonstrate his sincerity, the colonel arranged to fight a sham battle against a detachment of González's men. Guajardo easily won the "battle" and then had fifty-nine prisoners shot. Zapata decided to take a chance on the colonel's promise to defect because he desperately needed replacement soldiers and modern weapons.

An arrangement was made for Zapata to meet Colonel Guajardo at an abandoned hacienda. As Zapata and ten men approached the hacienda walls, the soldiers inside saluted him with a bugle call. One of the ten men riding with Zapata described the scene:

> Three times the bugle sounded the honor call, and as the last note died away, as [our leader] reached the door... the soldiers who were presenting arms fired two volleys, and our unforgettable General Zapata fell, never to rise again.

Emiliano Zapata was killed on the morning of April 10, 1919. His body, torn by scores of bullets, was carried on the back of a mule to the central square at the city of Cuautla. There it was tied to a post, where it remained for several days. Word passed from one tiny village to another that the beloved man the people called 'Miliano had been shot and that his body was on display.

Thousands of campesinos flocked from the countryside to see for themselves if this awful news was true. At Cuautla's square they saw him, lifeless, stiff, the blood caking on his white shirt. Still they refused to believe what they saw. Their 'Miliano could not die. He would march with the peasants and lead their army always, forever.

President Carranza was delighted when he heard that Zapata had been killed. He promoted Colonel González, the man who never won a battle, to the rank of general and gave him a bonus of 50,000 pesos.

In early 1920 Carranza's term of office was almost over. One of his strongest principles was no reelection of presidents,

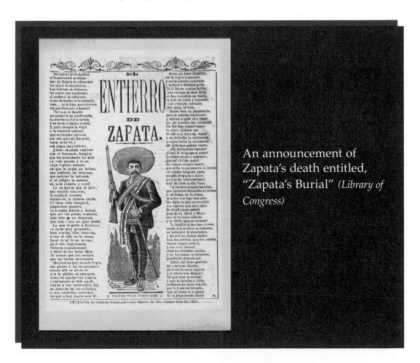

An announcement of Zapata's death entitled, "Zapata's Burial" *(Library of Congress)*

so he could not reasonably ask the public to give him another term. But Carranza was not a man to simply step down from a position of power. Before new elections were scheduled, he threw his support to a political unknown named Ignacio Bonillas, Mexico's ambassador to Washington. Bonillas had spent so much time in the United States that Mexicans joked that his name was not Senor Bonillas, but Mister Bonillas. It was clear to all what Carranza was trying to accomplish. He wanted Bonillas to become president and act as his puppet while he remained the real power behind the government.

Carranza, however, underestimated the influence and popularity enjoyed by his longtime rival Alvaro Obregón. Obregón felt he deserved the office of the president, and much of the Mexican public agreed. Because of Carranza's shady attempt to remain in power, Mexico was shaken by revolutionary armed force once again. In the state of Sonora, generals allied with Obregón declared rebellion and started marching their armies south. The marchers grew in number as more and

Ignacio Bonillas *(Library of Congress)*

In 1920, Alvaro Obregón rallied his rebel allies and marched to Mexico City to overthrow Carranza. *(Library of Congress)*

more generals joined the anti-Carranza crusade.

Fearing for his life, Carranza made plans to abandon Mexico City and travel to Veracruz, where he hoped to form a new government. With a staff that included cooks, servants, and a few loyal officers, Carranza boarded a twenty-one car train to make the journey. With him were sacks containing 5 million pesos in gold and silver which he had looted from the national treasury. He hoped to use it to pay soldiers and raise a new army.

The trip to Veracruz proved calamitous. The Carranza party became stranded in the state of Puebla because troops loyal to Obregón had blown up the train tracks. Forced to abandon the train, Carranza and his staff continued the journey on horseback.

At every remote mountain village, Carranza attracted a huge crowd, not because he was president but because in desperation he began giving away fistfuls of gold to any man willing to join his army. One soldier in the party recalled in amazement, "[The people] filled their pockets with gold, only to discover it was the worst possible thing they could have done because their horses were too loaded down to ride. And so they tried to rid themselves of the gold by giving it to everyone in their path. . . . It really is true what they tell you as a child . . . that money is worth nothing. It is truly worthless compared to saving your life."

As he fled over the rugged mountains of Puebla, Carranza paid a local chieftain named Rodolfo Herrera to protect him from his many enemies. Herrera assured the president he was safe in his region. He guided Carranza and his few remaining men to a remote mountain shack where he told the president he could get a good night's sleep. Exhausted, Carranza agreed to sleep in the shack, even though he preferred more comfortable quarters. During the night, Herrera, secretly an Obregón loyalist, shot and killed Carranza. Herrera later announced the president had committed suicide.

Once again a powerful army descended on Mexico City and marched down the Paseo de la Reforma. This time Mexico City dwellers did not cringe in fear. These were troops from Sonora, all of them loyal to Alvaro Obregón. Many Mexicans wept for joy when they saw the men. Even those who disliked Obregón recognized him as a no-nonsense political leader who would finally bring order to a nation torn asunder. Alvaro Obregón was not what the revolutionaries had demanded many bloody years ago, but he was the only leader with the political skills needed to usher in a new Mexico.

TEN

A New Society

lvaro Obregón was elected president in September of 1920. His ascendancy to the office marked the end of the warfare that had gripped the nation for ten years. Obregón was a practical politician, determined to bring peace to a battered land.

He continued Carranza's policy of demilitarization by rewarding generals if they agreed to disarm. This practice led to widespread corruption as many of the military strongmen were given government jobs. Once comfortably in office, the generals-turned-politicians raided the treasury as readily as they used to plunder rich haciendas.

In the north, Pancho Villa was bribed into dissolving his army with the gift of a 26,000-acre ranch. Enjoying life as a prosperous rancher, Villa became as greedy as the hacienda owners of the Díaz era. He hired thugs to gun down a group of peasants who tried to move onto the fringe areas of his land. Some of the slain campesinos were onetime members of Villa's own army.

On July 20, 1923, Pancho Villa was riding in a car through the town of Canutillo in northern Mexico. He was at the wheel and reportedly in a fine mood as he joked with other men in the auto. At a street corner an elderly man who sold candy from a stand raised his hand in salute and shouted out the old battle cry, "Viva Villa!" Pancho Villa waved to the old man, unaware that the salute and battle cry were a secret signal to a dozen or so hidden gunmen who waited, crouched below the windows of an apartment. Suddenly the vehicle was raked with rifle fire. Villa, hit at least ten times, died instantly. Some people claimed government agents were behind the murder, while others maintained Villa was shot by angry campesinos who coveted his ranch. The true reasons behind Villa's assassination remain unknown.

Upon hearing of Villa's shooting, President Obregón sent troops to Canutillo. He said he did so to prevent looting and violence from breaking out among Villa supporters. Other than that anti-looting measure, Villa's death did not affect the Obregón presidency.

On land reform, Obregón moved slowly. He established a legal process by which villagers could reclaim land taken from them by the haciendas, but the appeals of the peasants were often tied up for years in a cumbersome court system. Only in the state of Morelos, where the memory of Emiliano Zapata burned in the minds of militant farmers, did land reform proceed smoothly.

Reasoning that he would never be popular with small farmers, President Obregón established strong ties with the nation's labor movement. Many Mexican labor organizations were rotten with corruption. Union leaders pocketed dues paid by workers and accepted bribes from companies. Obregón dismissed bribery among union leaders as the hard price of peace.

Though the war had ended, violence was still common in Mexico. Militant Catholics battled in the streets with anticlerical revolutionaries. A growing Socialist and Communist movement urged mob action to steer Mexico on a more radical course. Also, many generals threatened to renew the war because they were unsatisfied with their rewards for disarming and were disappointed with what seemed to be a lack of any significant reform.

Obregón was harsh in dealing with upstart generals or radicals. Execution by firing squad was a common practice during his administration. The president had no love for summary executions, but he considered them necessary in a land still inflamed with revolutionary violence. "People are pacified with laws," he once said, "and laws are defended with rifles."

To his credit, Obregón launched a vigorous effort to educate all Mexican children. He also granted freedom of expression to artists and writers. The freedoms he unleashed stimulated a bold new society.

Obregón's supreme stroke of genius was the appointment of José Vasconcelos as secretary of education. A complex, intellectual and passionate man, Vasconcelos looked upon the education of Mexican youth as a holy crusade. Under his leadership money devoted to public education became the largest single item in the national budget for the first time in Mexico's history. Vasconcelos ordered more than one thousand new schools to be built, many in rural areas so primitive they lacked even a road. When groups of young men and women graduated from teachers' colleges, Vasconcelos himself gave them inspiring speeches and sent the young teachers marching into Mexico's hinterlands with the spirit of missionaries dispatched by the church.

Vasconcelos held a profound belief that literacy must become the birthright of all Mexicans. He established government printing houses and shipped millions of textbooks to the school systems. As a scholar, Vasconcelos favored the classics. So, soon after a child mastered rudimentary reading, he or she was given a copy of the works of Plato or Aristotle to study. Obregón, a purely practical man, thought that force feeding the classics to children who came from generations of illiterates was an exercise in folly. But the president gave Vasconcelos a free hand in his efforts to uplift the people.

José Vasconcelos Schools

Today there are dozens of schools throughout Mexico called *La Escuala de José Vasconcelos* (The José Vasconcelos School). The schools are named in honor of the outstanding minister of education who served in the 1920s.

Following Madero's precedent, Obregón freed the press from all censorship. In addition to newspapers, poetry magazines and theater groups were given liberty to lampoon and criticize the post-revolutionary government. The new spirit of freedom fostered a sparkling creative movement in Mexican literature. The war that had just concluded was the biggest and bloodiest event in the nation's history. Many of its participants—from the generals to the common soldiers—hungered

This mural painted by Diego Rivera depicts Zapata holding a "Land and Liberty" banner. *(Courtesy of Schalkwijk/Art Resource)*

to tell their part in this epic story. In the excitement of the new society, a flood of books poured forth.

One significant novel written about the Mexican Revolution was *Los de Abajo* (usually translated as *The Underdogs*), by Mariano Azuela. Azuela was a doctor who served with the army of Pancho Villa. His book tells the story of a simple peasant caught up in the whirlwind of revolutionary warfare. Initially the peasant has no clear idea why he is fighting. When the war degenerates into the general versus general stage, the man has become drunk on its mad violence: "Villa? Obregón? Carranza? What's the difference? I love the revolution like a volcano in eruption. I love the volcano because it's a volcano, the revolution because it's a revolution."

Azuela was disappointed with the results of the Mexican Revolution. Although the people had endured incredible suffering and loss of life, most were as poor now as they were before the war. Azuela concluded that Mexicans were betrayed by the Revolution's leaders because in the postwar years the leaders lived in luxury while the people struggled. To him the Mexican Revolution, like so many other wars in history, was

Mariano Azuela wrote *The Underdogs*, a novel about the Mexican Revolution.

one where the idealists were killed while the opportunists reaped rewards.

The Revolution also stimulated American journalism. Readers in the United States followed the movement of revolutionary armies with amazement, much as they would follow a football game. The American journalists who braved bullets and shells to bring the story home were hailed as heroes.

In 1914, the famous American writer Ambrose Bierce traveled to Mexico to write about the war. As a young man, Bierce had fought in the American Civil War. Since that awful experience, he was haunted by nightmare visions of corpses rotting on battlefields. Bierce's short stories were macabre tales that featured supernatural creatures and told of death in shocking terms. A line of Bierce's poetry goes, "What they

Ambrose Bierce

call dying/ is merely the last pain." Bierce was in his seventies when he traveled to Mexico. Somewhere in northern Mexico he disappeared, and neither his body nor his grave were ever discovered. Bierce simply faded away into legend. In 1985, the famous Mexican novelist Carlos Fuentes wrote a book about Ambrose Bierce titled *The Old Gringo*. The book later became a hit American movie starring Gregory Peck as Bierce.

Mexican art flourished in the postrevolutionary society. For generations talented Mexican painters had labored to copy the techniques used by the European masters. Then the Revolution caused a new pride to develop in the Mexican culture and spirit. Post-revolutionary art embraced exciting, purely Mexican themes. Paintings appeared showing villages where people ate tortillas instead of bread. The Mexican love for bright colors and wild forms burst out of canvasses. And the greatest of the post-revolutionary artists turned their attention to murals—an ancient Mexican tradition.

In pre-Columbian Mexico, Indian artists painted complex pictures on the walls of their temples and pyramids. After the Spanish Conquest the Indians, now joined with mestizo artists, painted stunning religious scenes inside Catholic churches. The Mexican muralist tradition flowered again in the 1920s. Education Secretary José Vasconcelos encouraged the mural movement by commissioning the best artists to paint the walls of public buildings. For Vasconcelos, this was a type of adult education: art told the visual story of the nation's history to people who could not read or write.

The three master muralists of the time were José Clemente Orozco, David Alfaro Siqueiros, and Diego Rivera. These "Big Three" painters became idols in Mexico. Critics around the world hailed their work as among the finest ever conceived on the American continent.

A revolution-themed mural painted by David Alfaro Siqueiros *(Courtesy of Schalkwijk/Art Resource)*

David Siqueiros was the youngest of the Big Three. He had served as an officer in the revolutionary army when he was still a teenager. A devoted Communist, he painted scenes of villagers who elevated themselves through their work and took an honored place in the modern industrial world. "I say we have had enough of pretty pictures of grinning peasants in traditional dress and carrying baskets on their backs," he said. "I say to hell with the ox carts—let's see more tractors and bulldozers." A fighter and rebel all his life, Siqueiros spent several years in jail for Communist activities. With a passion for politics as strong as his passion for art, he frequently ran off to attend political rallies, leaving many of his works unfinished.

Older and not so interested in politics was José Clemente Orozco. He grew up in Mexico City, and his early paintings showed a fascination with the capital's seedy nightlife. "Instead of red and yellow twilights I painted . . . drunken ladies and gentlemen," he once wrote. Many of Orozco's fellow painters tried to depict Mexico's revolution as a golden chapter in the country's history. To Orozco, however, the war was wasteful carnage. He was one of the many artists and writers who believed the Revolution's leaders had broken faith with the people. Orozco portrayed war as a horrific experience, never as a field of glory.

In the eyes of the Mexican public, Diego Rivera was the country's greatest artist. Beloved by the people, his antics in Mexico City nightclubs and his many love affairs were reported in detail in the national press. Rivera stood six feet tall and weighed a beefy three hundred pounds. Sporting an unkempt beard and usually wearing paint-stained clothes, he described himself as, "attractively ugly." Despite his

José Clemente Orozco working on a painting *(Courtesy of AP Images)*

tattered appearance, the artist had an almost magnetic effect on women. The most beautiful women in Mexican society and debutantes from Europe and the United States waited outside his studio in the hope that the great man would at least smile or say hello to them. Rivera, a womanizer by nature, had new girlfriends whenever he desired them. These romantic escapades infuriated Rivera's wife, Frida Kahlo, who was herself a brilliantly talented artist. Frida sometimes fought in public with Diego, but more often she smothered her sorrows by devoting herself to her work. Her paintings are now as famous as those of her husband.

Education Secretary Vasconcelos instructed the mural-

Frida Kahlo (left) stands beside her husband, Diego Rivera. *(Library of Congress)*

Frida Kahlo

When Frida Kahlo was eighteen she rode in a Mexico City bus when the driver lost control and the vehicle crashed. Frida was speared by a hand rail which penetrated her body. She endured many operations but was left in almost constant pain due to the accident. She turned her despair into artistic expression, rendering marvelous paintings which reflected her periods of agony followed by moments of happiness. Frida Kahlo was bedridden when her paintings were exhibited at an important gallery, and her loyal fans had to carry her in her bed to the exhibit. In 2002 the movie *Frida* was released. The film depicted her trials and stormy relations with her husband, Diego Rivera.

ists to concentrate on Mexican history as their primary theme for public buildings. Aside from this general direction, Vasconcelos gave the muralists the freedom to paint whatever they wished. Siqueiros preferred blatantly pro-Communist themes. Orozco glorified the historic meeting between Spaniards and Indians that created the mestizo race. Rivera, on the other hand, praised Indian civilization as a lost paradise and condemned the Spaniards as brutal slave masters.

The work of the muralists met with praise as well as with bitter denunciations. Mexico was still a nation at war with itself, even though no armies battled in the fields. When the muralists exalted communism or when they damned the Catholic Church, they touched on raw nerves. Some Mexico City residents, offended by the muralists' themes, threw rocks at the artists while they labored over their paintings. Art students defending the master muralists got into fistfights with outraged citizens. Yet the muralists—loved or hated for their works—remained national heroes for decades to come. When José Clemente Orozco died of a heart attack in 1949, thousands of people including Mexico City factory workers, waitresses, and taxi drivers wept on the streets.

ELEVEN

The Wake of War

Obregón's new society and the excitement generated by its literature and art could not cover up the wounds of war. Buildings in every city and village were reduced to rubble or pockmarked with bullet holes. Farms were in such a state of disruption that Mexico grew only one-tenth the amount of corn it needed to feed its people.

Worse was the war's tremendous cost in human lives. Perhaps as many as 2 million Mexicans—one in every eight of the population—had died either in battle or from the disease and famine brought about by warfare. The true number of deaths caused by the war is unknown, but government census figures give some indication of the enormous loss of life. The 1910 census gave Mexico a population of 15,160,369; in 1921 that number had dropped to 14,334,780. Traditionally, Mexico has a high birthrate. Yet, during the war years, the population was reduced by some 800,000 persons. The ten-year span from 1910 to 1920 was the only decade in modern Mexican history that saw the population decrease rather than rise. In terms of loss of life, the Mexican Revolution was the costliest war ever fought on the American continent, dwarfing even the great Civil War that took place in the United States.

People around the world wondered if Mexico reaped any benefits from this appallingly bloody war. On the surface it appeared the people gained nothing. Most campesinos remained landless. The nation as a whole was poorer than it was under Porfirio Díaz. Foreign observers concluded the Revolution was a waste. But subtle changes had crept into the nation's society as a result of the Revolution. The war broke the bonds of the past and altered the nation's mind and spirit. Gone was the caste system that separated Mexicans into whites, mestizos, and Indians and left many people—especially the Indians—aliens in their own land. Mexicans had suffered a period of horror and now emerged together hand in hand, like the survivors of a hurricane or an earthquake. The calamity of war assured that there would never again be a return to the old days. Though the Indians and the mestizos for the most part remained poorer than the whites, now all were Mexicans. After the war the nation was more unified than it had ever been before in its history.

Because the changes ushered in by the Revolution affected only Mexicans, the whole episode is a footnote rather than a headline in world history. The Russian Revolution of 1917 impacted the world because for a seventy-year period Communist leaders tried to export their insurrection to other nations. The American Revolution of 1776 and the French Revolution of 1789 fired the passions of liberty-loving people for centuries to come. The echoes of the Mexican

The Races of Mexico

Mexico is a multiracial society, and the issue of race is also complex. The vast majority of people in Mexico are mestizos, meaning mixed race. But the country is also home to *indios*, (Indians, the indigenous people of Mexico), *negros*, (blacks, tens of thousands of whom were brought by the Spanish as slaves), and whites. White is generally used to describe Spaniards, and any non-Spanish whites are generally labeled by nationality rather than race: American, German, British, etc.

Revolution—though they were profound—stayed at home, appreciated mostly by the people of Mexico.

The Mexican philosopher Octavio Paz claims the Revolution was a hammer blow that enabled Mexico to shatter the almost feudal society it maintained in the past and complete its rise to become a modern state. In his book *The Labyrinth of Solitude*, Paz explains, "Our Revolution is the other face of Mexico. . . . It is the brutal, resplendent face of death and fiestas, of gossip and gunfire . . . And with whom does Mexico commune in this bloody fiesta? With herself, with her own being. Mexico dares to exist, to be. The revolutionary explosion is a prodigious fiesta in which the Mexican, drunk with his own self, is aware at last, in a mortal embrace, of his fellow Mexican."

Postwar politics remained turbulent, but at least a semblance of order prevailed. Obregón's term of office expired in 1924, and Plutarco Elias Calles was elected president. When Calles took office, it marked the first peaceful change of presidents that Mexico had experienced in more than

Plutarco Elias Calles was elected president of Mexico in 1924.

forty years. During the war, Calles had been an Obregón's supporter. As president he continued Obregón's policies, especially the program to build schools in rural areas. But Calles lacked Obregón's charm and sense of humor. He interpreted criticism from the press or from political opponents as personal insults. Calles also harbored an intense hatred toward the Catholic Church.

Throughout the revolutionary years most leaders claimed to be anticlerical, but their stance often left a bitter taste in the mouths of their followers. Mexico was a deeply religious society, and the vast majority were (and still are) devoted Catholics. President Calles pushed the Mexican conscience too far when he deported one hundred priests and nuns and closed all the nation's remaining religious schools. To protest these actions, the Catholic Church went on strike in 1926. Church leaders ordered priests not to celebrate Mass, perform marriages, or render any other church services. The strike lasted for three years, and during that time, not one church bell chimed in Mexico. The absence of bells deeply saddened people of farming communities; traditionally, church bells control the rhythm of Mexican village life. They gently wake the people in the morning, call them to Mass on Sundays, and announce weddings and deaths. Then suddenly they were silent.

Because of Calles's repression of the church, a short lived uprising called the Cristero Rebellion broke out in 1927. Crying out *"Viva Cristo Rey!"* ("Long Live Christ the King!"), the Cristeros burned government schools and murdered officials. Calles sent the army to crush the rebellion. Hundreds of Cristeros were hanged from telephone poles. This was one of the last periods of violence in the revolutionary period.

Calles's term expired in 1928, and Alvaro Obregón, noting that the constitution only barred immediate reelection after the completion of a term, ran again for the office of president. He was still a popular leader and was again elected. Three weeks after the election, Obregón ate dinner with friends at a suburban Mexico City restaurant. A young, well-dressed man with a sketch pad drew pictures of several guests in the Obregón party. The artist asked the president-elect if he could draw him, too. Obregón agreed. He had no idea the artist was a Catholic fanatic who hated Obregón because he had made many anticlerical speeches. The artist pulled a pistol from his jacket and fired five times into Obregón's face. The president-elect died instantly.

Just a few years earlier, an incident such as Obregón's assassination would have thrown the country into renewed revolution. But the peace was unbroken. Working within the system set up by the constitution and former President Calles, a succession of three presidents held office, each serving a two-year term. They were mere puppets of Calles, and

Mexicans called them "straw men." Then, in 1934, a state governor named Lázaro Cárdenas was elected president.

Cárdenas was a teenager when the Mexican Revolution broke out. He organized a band of soldiers and joined Obregón's army. As president he displayed a commitment to the poor never before seen in a Mexican political leader. He routinely rode burro-back to the nation's most remote areas to listen to the problems faced by the farmers.

In 1938, Cárdenas shocked the financial world by nationalizing Mexico's oil, thereby claiming all oil fields to be the property of the state. This action infuriated American companies, but Mexicans were overjoyed by the president's boldness.

Cárdenas had bolstered his reputation as a defender of the revolution by implementing a land reform policy that distributed ejido land to many of the nation's peasants. During his term in office, he redistributed more hacienda

Lázaro Cárdenas (right) was elected president of Mexico in 1934 and went on to become what many historians consider to be the greatest Mexican president of the twentieth century. *(Courtesy of AP Images)*

land to the villagers than all other Mexican presidents combined.

By the end of Lázaro Cárdenas's term of office in 1940, memories of the great upheaval had faded. Children learned of

---

Cuauhtémoc Cárdenas

The adoration the Mexican people felt for Lázaro Cárdenas spanned the decades. His son, Cuauhtémoc Cárdenas, was a popular political leader in the 1980s and 1990s. He was born in Mexico City in 1934 and was named Cuauhtémoc by his father after the last of the Aztec chieftains. Cuauhtémoc ran for president of Mexico three times. Many Mexicans believe he actually won the 1988 contest but he was robbed of the office due to vote fraud.

---

the Revolution from stories told by their grandparents. Also, revolutionary deeds were celebrated in fiestas. During fiesta time, children, dressed as soldiers, re-fought battles in the village square while rockets burst overhead. Aging soldiers and soldaderas smiled at the mock combat.

The fiestas brought long-dead heroes back to life. A boy dressed as Pancho Villa would be chased around the square by another boy dressed as American General Pershing. Always the Pancho Villa character escaped. A boy or girl wearing a stovepipe hat typical of a revolutionary era politician would recite a speech that was once delivered by the martyred President Madero. The fiesta audience applauded the child's effort, even if the child stumbled over the words.

The mere mention of one revolutionary figure—Emiliano Zapata—silenced even the wildest fiesta. Unselfish, completely devoted to his followers, and fearless in battle, Zapata is regarded as the upheavel's greatest leader. So heroic is the spirit of the man that among the campesinos in the south he never really died. Years after the Revolution ended farmers claimed they still saw him mounted on a white horse and riding over the ranch lands he loved—always he rode alone. People young and old bowed their heads in deep respect, upon hearing Zapata's name. Then, together, the Mexican people, aware of the decades of violence and struggle in their past, and filled with pride over the sacrifices of the leaders who gave everything for their nation, throw themselves back into the thrill and celebration of the fiesta. They celebrate the freedom in the present, and work as a unified nation—a Mexico for and made of Mexicans—to build the future.

Timeline

1909 Porfirio Díaz has ruled as president for most of the previous thirty-three years, bringing factories and a modern railroad system to Mexico, but his policies allow land-rich haciendas to expand at the expense of village ejidos; despite industrial progress, most Mexicans remain impoverished and uneducated.

1910 April—Francisco Madero enters the presidential race, becoming the first serious opposition that Díaz has ever faced.

June—Díaz has Madero jailed on trumped-up charges; Díaz wins the presidential election.

October—Madero, released from jail, announces Plan of San Luis Potosi; Plan declares Díaz election to be illegal, calls for Mexicans to rebel on November 20.

November—Rebellion urged by Madero fails to take place; two separate armed revolutions break out in the north and the south—in the north, Pancho Villa's army begins raiding rich cattle ranches, in the south peasant leader Emiliano Zapata rallies landless farmers, takes over large haciendas.

1911 May—Pancho Villa captures Ciudad Juárez, allowing Villa to supply army with weapons purchased in the United States; Díaz resigns from office, leaves Mexico for exile in France.

October—Madero wins in first free election in decades.

November—Emiliano Zapata issues the Plan of Ayala, calling for return of all village land taken illegally by haciendas.

1912 March—Pascual Orozco, a former ally of Pancho Villa, begins rebellion against Madero; Madero chooses General Victoriano Huerta to defeat Orozco. June–July—Madero is criticized by press and other revolutionaries.

1913 February—The Tragic Ten Days begin in Mexico City; thousands die from artillery bombardments, as General Felix Díaz, nephew of Porfirio Díaz, tries to force Madero out of office; United States ambassador Henry Lane Wilson helps to arrange secret meetings between Felix Díaz and General Huerta; Madero is murdered; Huerta assumes command of Mexico. October–November—Rebel armies gather under Pancho Villa, Carranza, and Obregón; war against Huerta begins.

1914 April—American Marines occupy port city Veracruz. July—Huerta resigns, leaves Mexico. August—Mexico City occupied first by armies of Obregón and Carranza, then by armies of Villa and Zapata.

1915 February—Obregón and Carranza reoccupy Mexico City; Carranza assumes political leadership over the nation; rival generals clash. April—Obregón's army defeats Villa's at Battle of Celaya. October—U.S. President Woodrow Wilson recognizes Carranza as official president of Mexico, infuriating Pancho Villa.

1916 Pancho Villa and five hundred followers cross

American border, raid the city of Columbus, New Mexico, killing sixteen Americans; President Wilson sends army under General John Pershing into Mexico with orders to capture Villa alive or dead.

1917 January—General Pershing withdraws from Mexico after ten months, unable to capture Pancho Villa.
February—New constitution approved; constitution calls for the separation of church and state, and guarantees rights for workers.
March—Carranza officially elected president of Mexico.

1918 Emiliano Zapata organizes separate society in southern Mexico; Zapatistas redistribute land by dividing hacienda properties; Carranza sends army units to defeat Zapatista movement.

1919 Zapata tricked into attending a secret meeting with a Carranza general and is murdered.

1920 May—President Carranza killed near the city of Veracruz.
September—Obregón elected president of Mexico.

Sources

CHAPTER ONE: Messages from the Gods

p. 13-14, "an excess and a squandering . . ." Octavio Paz, *The Labyrinth of Solitude* (New York: Grove Press, 1985), 148.

CHAPTER TWO: The Díaz Years

p. 19, "Kill them on the spot," T. R. Fehrenbach, *Fire and Blood: A History of Mexico* (New York: Macmillan Publishing Co., 1973), 452.

p. 19, "A dog with a bone . . ." Ibid., 460.

p. 28, "by the sixth or seventh . . ." Jonathan Kandell, *La Capital: The Biography of Mexico City* (New York: Henry Holt and Company, 1990), 367.

p. 29, "It's twenty cutters . . ." B. Traven, *The Rebellion of the Hanged* (New York: Alfred A. Knopf, 1953 edition), 94.

p. 30, "He pacified and united . . ." Adolpho Gilly, *The Mexican Revolution* (New York and London: The New Press, 2005), 39.

p. 31, "Mexico—mother of foreigners . . ." Anita Brenner, *The Wind That Swept Mexico* (Austin: University of Texas Press, 1973), 24.

p. 31-32, "Nothing is just or unjust . . ." Kandell, *La Capital*, 374.

p. 32, "The weak, the unprepared . . ." Ibid., 374.

p. 33, "A revolution in Mexico . . ." Eduardo Ruiz Ramon, *The Great Rebellion: Mexico 1905-1924* (New York: W.W. Norton, 1980), 9.

CHAPTER THREE: The Gathering Storm

p. 36, "No matter what my friends . . ." Kandell, *La Capital*, 390.

p. 41, "Thousands thronged . . . without applause," Ibid., 395.

p. 45, "These are difficult times . . ." Ibid., 404.

p. 45, "Here is one rich . . ." Martin Luis Guzman, *Memoirs of Pancho Villa*, trans. Virginia H. Taylor (Austin: University of Texas Press, 1966), 38.

p. 48, "Little work, lots of . . ." William Weber Johnson, *Heroic Mexico: The Violent Emergence of a Modern Nation* (New York: Doubleday, 1968), 65.

p. 49, "They [the revolutionaries] have turned . . ." Ibid., 69.

p. 50, "Quando Madero llego . . ." Enrique Krauze, *Mexico: Biography of Power,* trans. Hank Heifetz (New York: Harper Collins, 1996), 260.

CHAPTER FOUR: Madero

p. 53, "The Mexican people are not asking . . ." Hudson Strode, *Timeless Mexico* (New York: Harcourt Brace, 1944), 228.

p. 55, "This little man . . ." Gilly, *The Mexican Revolution*, 69.

p. 55, "But why don't you . . ." Johnson, *Heroic Mexico*, 80.

p. 57, "If they resist me . . ." Kandell, *La Capital*, 408.

p. 58, "we declare that . . ." Gilly, *The Mexican Revolution*, 71.

p. 59, "What remains for us . . ." Kandell, *La Capital*, 410.

p. 59, "seething with discontent . . ." Henry Bamford Parkes, *A History of Mexico* (Boston: Houghton Mifflin Company, 1988), 330.

p. 59, "There is no peace . . ." Anita Brenner, *The Wind That Swept Mexico* (Austin: University of Texas Press, 1973), 33.

CHAPTER FIVE: The Tragic Ten Days

p. 69, "It was a spectacle . . ." Kandell, *La Capital*, 413.

p. 70-71, "Oh, Mr. Madero will be . . ." Ibid., 417.

p. 71, "Mexico has been . . ." Lesley Bird Simpson,
Many Mexicos (Berkeley and Los Angeles: University
of California Press, 1966), 300.

CHAPTER SIX: Huerta

p. 77, "I do not deny . . ." Guzman, *Memoirs of Pancho Villa*,
284.

p. 82, "It is good, fighting . . ." William Weber Johnson,
Life World Library: Mexico (New York: Time, Incorporated,
1964), 59.

p. 82, "I am going to teach . . ." Fehrenbach, *Fire and Blood*,
514.

p. 84, "I saw an uncommon . . ." Gilly, *The Mexican
Revolution*, 345.

CHAPTER SEVEN: War Consumes Mexico

p. 87, "For me the war began . . ." Johnson, *Heroic Mexico*,
157.

p. 90, "He is the most . . ." Krauze, *Mexico: Biography
of Power*, 116.

p. 93, "Men of the south . . ." Strode, *Timeless Mexico*, 259.

p. 94, "Emiliano, what do you . . ." Ibid., 298.

p. 95, "The task of establishing peace . . ." Brenner, *The
Wind That Swept Mexico*, 40.

p. 96, "fiesta of bullets," Paz, *The Labyrinth of Solitude*,
148.

p. 99, "In the bloody . . ." Guzman, *Memoirs of Pancho Villa*,
168.

CHAPTER EIGHT: General Versus General

p. 102, "It was inexcusable . . ." Kandell, *La Capital*, 429.

p. 103, "Since I Know how . . ." Ibid., 429.

p. 108, "What I can't get . . ." Mariano Azuela, *The*

Underdogs, trans. E. Mungia Jr. (New York: New American Library, 1962 edition), 133.

p. 116, "No one can follow me . . ." Krauze, *Mexico: Biography of Power*, 329-330.

p. 116, "Did the Americans think . . ." Gilly, *The Mexican Revolution*, 226.

CHAPTER NINE: Twilight of the Generals

p. 122, "The lands and waters . . ." Gilly, *The Mexican Revolution*, 234.

p. 122-123, "From the time you first . . ." Johnson, *Heroic Mexico*, 331.

p. 124, "Three times the bugle . . . " Kandell, *La Capital*, 439.

p. 128, "[The people] filled . . ." Ibid., 441.

CHAPTER TEN: A New Society

p. 131, "People are pacified . . ." Johnson, *Heroic Mexico*, 370.

p. 133-134, "Villa? Obregon? Carranza?" Azuela, *The Underdogs*, 133.

p. 134-135, "What they call . . ." Carlos Fuentes, *The Old Gringo*, trans. Margaret Sayers Peden (New York:Farrar, Straus, Giroux, 1985), 2.

p. 137, "I say we have . . ." Anne Horan and David S. Thomson, ed., *Mexico* (Alexandria, Virginia: Time-Life Books, 1986), 128.

p. 137, "Instead of red and yellow . . ." Ibid., 129.

CHAPTER ELEVEN: The Wake of War

p. 143, "Our Revolution is the . . ." Paz, *The Labyrinth of Solitude*, 148-149.

Bibliography

Brandenberg, Frank. *The Making of Modern Mexico.* Englewood Cliffs, N.J.: Prentice Hall, 1964.

Brenner, Anita. *The Wind That Swept Mexico.* Austin, Tex.: University of Texas Press, 1943.

Cumberland, Charles. *Mexican Revolution (The Constitutionalist Years).* Austin, Tex.: University of Texas Press, 1974.

Fehrenbach, T.R. *Fire and Blood: A History of Mexico.* New York: Macmillan Publishing Co., 1973.

Kandell, Jonathan. *La Capital: The Biography of Mexico City.* New York: Random House, 1988.

Knight, Man. *The Mexican Revolution, Vols. 1 and 2.* London: Cambridge University Press, 1986.

Parkes, Henry Bamford. *A History of Mexico.* Boston: Houghton Mifflin Co., 1938.

Reed, John. *Insurgent Mexico.* New York: International Publishers, 1984.

Ruiz, Ramon Eduardo. *The Great Rebellion, Mexico: 1905–1924.* New York: W. W. Norton Co., 1980.

Turner, John Kenneth. *Barbarous Mexico.* Austin, Tex.: University of Texas Press, 1969.

Wilkie, James W., and Albert Michaels. *Revolution in Mexico: Years of Upheaval, 1910-1940.* Tucson, Ariz.: University of Arizona Press, 1984.

Womack, John, Jr. *Zapata and the Mexican Revolution.* New York: Alfred A. Knopf, 1969.

Web Sites

http://www.elpasotexas.gov/mcad/mexicanrevolution/history.asp

In 2010, the city of El Paso, in Texas, and Ciudad Juarez, in Mexico, will join together to celebrate the centennial of the Mexican Revolution. This site is maintained by the City of El Paso Museum and Cultural Affairs Department, and it features an article on the history of the Revolution, updates on the countdown to the 2010 celebration, and images from the Revolution.

http://runyon.lib.utexas.edu/conflict.html

The University of Texas at Austin is home to an extensive collection of photographs taken by border photographer Robert Runyon during the Revolution. The 350 images document what Runyon witnessed in Matamoros, Monterrey, Ciudad Victoria, and the Texas border area and surrounding area.

http://historicaltextarchive.com/sections.php?op= listarticles&secid=30

Twenty-nine articles on various aspects of the Mexican Revolution can be found on this Web site, which was created by a university professor. Written primarily by historians, each article has an extensive notes and bibliography section.

Index